# BREAKING THE
# TAX
# CODE
## SECOND EDITION

Published by CelebrityPress™, Orlando, FL
A division of The Celebrity Branding Agency®
Celebrity Branding® is a registered trademark
Printed in the United States of America.

ISBN: 9780983947028
LCCN: 2011937851

This publication is designed to provide accurate and authoritative
information with regard to the subject matter covered. It is sold with
the understanding that the publisher is not engaged in rendering legal,
accounting, or other professional advice. If legal advice or other expert assistance is required, the services of a competent professional should be sought. The opinions expressed by the authors in this book are not endorsed by CelebrityPress™ and are the sole responsibility of the author rendering the opinion.

Most CelebrityPress™ titles are available at special quantity discounts for bulk purchases for sales promotions, premiums, fundraising, and educational use. Special versions or book excerpts can also be created to fit specific needs.

For more information, please write:
CelebrityPress™, 520 N. Orlando Ave, #2
Winter Park, FL 32789

or call 1.877.261.4930

Visit us online at www.CelebrityPressPublishing.com

# BREAKING THE

# TAX

# CODE

## SECOND EDITION

AMERICA'S LEADING TAX PROFESSIONALS
REVEAL PROVEN STRATEGIES TO LEGALLY

# MINIMIZE
# YOUR TAXES

AND KEEP MORE OF WHAT YOU EARN

# Table of Contents

# Foreword

In my years of working with thousands of tax and accounting professionals across the United States and Canada, I've seen many kinds. Of course, there is the standard stereotype of the pencil-pushing numbers geek – with all of the personality of a thumbtack, and the communication skills that go along with it.

And sure, we want our tax professionals to be wonky, and we want them to be excellent at keeping up with the tax code (which is a weekly endeavor, with Congressional maneuverings being what they are).

But as a small business owner (who has fired his share of poorly-performing accountants and bookkeepers), and a father of young children, I've learned to place an emphasis on those tax accountants who not only can control the tax code like a lion tamer ... but who are pro-active about communication, consultation and **relationship.**

There are very good reasons why most tax accountants are terrible at this basic business, and life skill. Most fly through tax season, hopped-up on caffeine and navigating through a blizzard of forms, paperwork, staff concerns and client requests.

But the authors in this book have made a commitment, over the years, to set up systems within their firms which enable them to find **creative solutions for just about any kind of tax or accounting conundrum in which a family or business owner might find themselves.**

They are all leaders who proved their worth, got good at what they do, and most importantly, are willing to share it with you. All of them came from ordinary backgrounds, but yet have created relationships (and **results**) for their clients which transcend the ordinary, and truly create financial well-being for generations.

This book is full of leaders in the accounting and tax field who've 'been there, done that' and come out on top – despite all the 'dream stealers' trying to take them down. They are survivors, many overcoming large obstacles, both physical and financial, and a few mental roadblocks as well.

The lessons in this book would take years to learn – possibly a lifetime or maybe never. Reading it is like sitting in the middle of a table in a brainstorming meeting attended by some of the best minds in tax accounting.

I'd consider you lucky to have discovered this book. Sit down in a quiet place and get to know your authors, and when you're finished, rest with the confidence that yes, the tax "code" can, in fact, be broken.

Here's to financial peace for you, your family and/or your business,

Nate Hagerty
*Small Business Owner, Coach and Friend To Thousands of Tax Accountants in North America*

# CHAPTER 1

# The Unique World of Clergy Taxation

By Linda Cochran

## What is so unique about clergy's income taxes?

*1. DUAL-STATUS Tax Treatment:*
Dual-Status means that they are an employee for income tax reporting and fringe benefits and as self-employed for social security purposes. To qualify for the unique Dual-Status tax treatment, an employee of a church or an integral agency of a church must be performing ministerial duties. These duties include preaching, teaching, evangelism, conduct of worship, administration, baptisms, weddings, funerals, and communions. No other taxpayer has a dual-status tax treatment. Their employer is not required to withhold federal, social security, medicare, or state income tax from their wages. But it is optional if the clergy employee and the employer agree to it. They are to receive a W-2 reporting their wages to the IRS and not a 1099 because they are a "common law" employee. If their employer does not withhold these taxes for them then they are required to pay their taxes quarterly, just like any other self-employed tax payer.

*2. Social Security Exemption:*
They have the opportunity to become exempt from paying the Social Security tax on their ministerial earnings by timely fil-

ing form 4361 and having it approved by the IRS. The 4361 says that because of your religious principles, you are conscientiously opposed to accepting, for services performed as a member of the clergy, any public insurance (governmental insurance that makes payments in the event of death, disability, old age, or retirement). Public insurance includes insurance systems established by the Social Security Act. Once this election is made is it irrevocable unless they have a change of faith or unless Congress opens a window of time to revoke this decision. Beginning with the date they are hired, they have a two year window to obtain this exemption. This two year window is until the due date (April 15th) of their tax return, including extensions (October 15th), for the second year in which they have net self-employment clergy earnings of $400 or more. A change of faith happens when there is a change in denominations or they go from one autonomous to another autonomous church.

### *3. Tax-Free Housing Allowance:*
The clergy also qualify for Tax-Free Housing (Parsonage/Rental) Allowance. It includes anything spent to provide a home for the clergy and their family. It includes the expenses for the house, its contents, the garage, and the yard. Even the garbage bags and the light bulbs are included in the housing allowance. Housing allowance is free from income tax, but subject to social security and medicare tax. The housing allowance is only exempt for federal and state income tax. It is subject to the self-employment tax (social security and medicare tax).

### *4. Housing Allowance Designation:*
The housing allowance must be officially designated ahead of time (before being paid) to the clergy. It needs to be a specific amount or a specific percentage of the clergy's salary. It could even be 100 percent of their salary. It is limited to the lower of the amount officially designated, the amount actually used to provide a home, or the fair rental value of the home, the furnishings, and the utilities.

## 5. Unbelievable Tax Shelter:

The clergy get a double deduction of the home mortgage interest and property taxes on their home. They can deduct these even though the mortgage is paid with nontaxable income. Many clergy end up not paying any federal income tax using the housing allowance rule and the double deduction of the home interest and property taxes. They would then just be subject to the social security and medicare tax unless they have become exempt from that tax.

## 6. Retirement Savings Accounts:

They are entitled to put their retirement dollars into a 401(a), 401(k), 403(b), 408(k), or a 408(p) plan. During their working years, when these dollars are going into this plan, they are not subject to federal, state, or social security and medicare tax. When they retire, they can withdraw these dollars tax-free by having them designated as parsonage allowance (to the extent spent for housing) by their former employer or by the pension board of their denomination. At this time, this income would not be subject to federal, state, or social security and medicare tax.

## 7. Tax Free Retirement Gratuity Payments to Retired Clergy (based on age or disability):

Payments made by a church to the retired clergy that are based on appreciation and gratitude, and are not required by an established plan entered into before their retirement, are considered non-taxable gifts.

## About Linda

Linda Cochran is one of **Michigan's Premier Tax Accountants** and is a **"tax savings and tax resolution expert."** She is persistent with the IRS (she doesn't back down from the IRS or take no for an answer if she is convinced she is right), knowledgeable, and experienced. She has been an accountant for over 30 years. Her office and staff is in Flint, Michigan where she serves several hundred accounting and tax clients.

Over the years, Linda has advised hundreds of small businesses how to save thousands of dollars in taxes by using strategy and tax deductions that they simply were not aware of. Her ultimate joy in life is using her skills helping people who are unequipped to help themselves when it comes to taxes and accounting.

She is also a published author of: *Fighting Back! How To Pay The IRS On Your Terms!*

Contact Information:
Cochran Tax Service, Inc.
2501 S. Dye Rd., Ste. C
Flint, MI 48532
Phone: 810-720-5520
Fax: 810-720-5520
Web: cochrantax.com
E-mail:linda@cochrantaxservice.com

# CHAPTER 2

# The Importance Of Choosing The Right Business Entity

## By Richard B. Soscia, MBA, CFP, DABFA

### INTRODUCTION:

As a leader in entrepreneurship, business operations, accounting, tax, finance, economics, and business intelligence, I have assisted many clients of varies sizes and industries understand the dynamics of their business and the most advantageous structure in which to operate. Whether they are starting a business or are presently in business, there are many important decisions that must be made that will affect their personal and business finances for years to come. One of those choices is deciding their business entity. The type of entity they choose for their business can provide them with significant tax, legal and business advantages. A wide variety of business entities (forms of doing business) have been devised and our website (www.summitfinservices.com) provides a detailed comparison of corporate and non-corporate attributes. Because of the importance of selecting the appropriate entity, it is an important subject to consider. As additional forms of doing business have been devised, the Internal Revenue Service has kept up by issuing tax rules for these entities.

The IRS has basically developed two Federal Tax Systems for businesses:

1. Taxation of both the entity itself and the owners, and

2. "Pass-through" taxation.

Although only two Federal Tax Systems exist for businesses, within the systems are various types of business entities and each has significant tax advantages depending on the type of business, its purpose, mission and vision. For business purposes, these involve corporate entities and unincorporated entities. In this chapter, we will review the tax implications of the main entity types considering net income, dividends and wages.

## 1. CORPORATE Entities:

It is generally agreed by both tax and legal professionals, that if your business is not incorporated, you may be throwing away thousands of dollars in tax savings and deductions. A corporation is a legal entity that exists separately from its owners. All corporations start as "C" corporations and provide the benefit of liability protection, tax advantages, and ease in raising capital.

The tax benefit is that a corporation can be structured many ways to provide substantial tax savings. This includes minimizing self-employment taxes, increasing allowable deductions and providing tax credits that lower the taxes paid on net income. Many corporations structure retirement plans, tax-deferred savings plans and many other plans for both their owners and employees, which provide even greater tax savings. Because the corporation is separate from its owners, its life is unlimited, ownership is easily transferable, capital can be raised through the sale of stock and management is centralized. The corporation is responsible for paying its own taxes on its income and any loss is carried forward to offset future income. Two main exceptions to this rule are that a distribution of dividends from the corporation are not deductible by the corporation but are included as income by the owners, and the sale of appreciated property by the corporation with proceeds going to the owners can result in double taxation. Therefore, paying strict attention to these and other areas will ensure that taxes are minimized to both the corporation and its owners.

While all corporations start out as "C" corporations, they can easily become "S" corporations. Many stockholders choose the tax treatment of an "S" corporation because the net income or loss is "passed-through" to the shareholders and are included in their personal tax returns. This provides a benefit if the stockholders calculate losses in the initial years of operations or because the combined income will result in a lower tax obligation. Moreover, a distribution to the stockholders from the retained profits in the corporation is not taxed and the "pass-through" of net earnings does not result in Social Security or Medicare taxes. The net income, as well as certain other types of income, gains and losses, is reported to the shareholders based on percentage interest in the corporation. However, certain types of deductions, plans and credits are either not allowed in an "S" corporation or are not allowed to the more than 2% stockholders of an "S" corporation. These shareholders, if they receive wages from the corporation, can claim certain deductions on their personal return. Moreover, as the business grows and more capital is required, a corporation can easily change back to a "C" corporation. This is important because an "S" corporation is only allowed 100 shareholders, and must use a calendar year-end unless otherwise approved by the IRS.

## 2. UNINCORPORATED Entities:

An unincorporated entity is an entity that has the same characteristics as a company but is not incorporated. It is also sometimes called a voluntary association because the individuals in such an entity choose to associate and the entity does not exist separately from the individuals. Accordingly, unincorporated entities are all considered "pass-through" entities because all gains or losses pass to the individual, partners or members. The primary unincorporated entities are:

1. Sole proprietorship (individual)
2. Partnerships of various types (partners)
3. Limited Liability entities (members)

While a sole proprietorship is an unincorporated entity, it is not generally selected as a business entity because it only involves one individual and does not present any real tax advantage.

Ordinary partnerships, called "general partnerships" do not have limited liability under state law. Limited partnerships limit liability for some partners but not others. A limited partnership has both general partners, who manage the business and limited partners, who are passive investors. A limited partner's liability is generally limited to his/her investment. A general partner's liability is unlimited unless the general partner is an LLP. In all cases, the partnership is a pass-through entity and all profits, revenue and deductions pass through to the partners, who report their share on their individual tax returns. Therefore, the profits are only taxed once (at the personal level of its owners) rather than twice, as is the case with corporations, which are taxed at the corporate level and then again at the personal level when dividends are distributed to the shareholders. The benefits of single taxation can also be secured by forming a limited liability company (a new hybrid of corporations and partnerships that is still evolving). Partnership net income is subject to Social Security and Medicare as well as income tax. It should be noted that a general partnership in which the partners are husband and wife is reported on Schedule C of Form 1040.

Limited Liability Companies (LLCs) have become the most popular business form for new entities, and many existing entities have converted to this form. The LLC combines limited liability with pass-through tax treatment and can offer benefits unavailable from "S" corporations. These include:

1. *Allocating certain tax benefits disproportionately among owners;*
2. *Opportunity for greater loss deductions; and,*

*3.Avoiding or reducing tax when a new owner joins the business or when distributions are made to owners in business liquidation.*

A single member LLC (SMLLC) can be either a corporation or a single member "disregarded entity" (Sole Proprietor). To be treated under Federal Law as a Corporation, The SMLLC has to file Form 8832 and elect to be classified as a corporation. An SMLLC that does not elect to be a corporation will be classified by the existing federal guidance as a "disregarded entity" which is taxed as a sole proprietor for income tax purposes. Also businesses in banking, trust, and insurance industries are prohibited from forming LLCs.

However, since 1997, the IRS has allowed business owners a previously unheard-of measure of choices as to how the entity will be federally taxed. Using Form 8832 greatly simplifies the once complicated process of allowing the LLC members to elect how they would like their entity to be treated for tax purposes. Both single and multiple member LLCs may use the form. Though most often multiple-member LLCs wish to be treated as an S corporation or partnership in order to benefit from the pass-through taxation, this should not automatically be assumed, as ideally, members of all tax-classifications of LLCs may be best-served by filing form 8832 as an affirmative selection of the manner in which they want their entity to be taxed.

LLCs with more than one member are usually classified as a partnership for tax treatment purposes, though it is not mandated. A multiple-member LLC can elect to be treated as a "C" or "S" corporation, but it would lose the pass-through taxation benefits afforded the partnership tax treatment with "C" corporation tax treatment, and is limited with respect to how many members it can have and prevents non-citizen/resident alien ownership with the "S" corporation taxation. Subject to the subchapter K of the Internal Revenue Code governing the taxation of partners and partnerships, electing to have your LLC taxed as a partnership would subject it only to a single Federal Income Tax at the partner level, with each member reporting his share of each item in the LLC's gain, loss, income, deduction, or credit on his personal tax return.

The restrictions on the equity and capital structure of an "S" corporation can significantly limit the flexibility in strategic planning for your company, especially for growth, changes in stock types, inter-generational business transfers, etc. Among these restrictions, for example, are the limitation that an "S" corporation can have no more than 100 shareholders, and that shareholders can only be individuals and estates (some trusts, but not other corporations). Another limitation is that an "S" corporation can only issue one class of stock, thus limiting one of the LLC's flexibilities in that it can have varying levels of ownership interest.

Professional service organizations originally were incorporated as a "Professional Corporation" (P.C.). These provided limited liability for general business debts but not for the professional's own malpractice and, in some states, no limited liability for malpractice of fellow practitioners in the firm. Now most professional organizations use Limited Liability Partnerships (LLPs). LLPs are general partnerships whose general partners have limited liability. A partner is liable for his/her own malpractice but not for a partner's malpractice or, depending on state law, other acts of partners. Typically, under state law they are required to maintain malpractice insurance, and are obliged to pay a per partner fee to keep their status, but are not subject to entity-level tax.

## 3. CHOOSING THE FORM:

After discussing the various forms of business, you must decide which form will work best for your business, and capitalize on its profits or startup losses. A decision of whether to use a "C" corporation is sometimes necessary from a business standpoint. From a tax standpoint, while a "C" corporation presents two levels of tax, the first tax on the corporation can be at a lower rate than the tax on the owner, and the owner can benefit from a number of fringe benefits that will lower the tax rate even further and postpone dividends or other assets from being distributed to the owner. A "C" corporation is not a preferable choice for a new business.

An "S" corporation limitation of liability gives it an edge for business purposes over general partnerships and sole proprietorships. However, "S" corporations are subject to a number of significant rules and restrictions:

1. *All owners must agree to "S" corp. status. This means that one co-owner can exact a price or impose conditions for his or her agreement.*

2. *An "S" corp. can have only one class of stock, which means that income, losses and other tax attributes are allotted among stockholders in proportion to stock ownership.*

3. *The number of co-owners is limited (to 100, with qualifications, counting members of the same family as one stockholder).*

4. *There are limitations as to who can be co-owners (for example, a nonresident alien cannot) and as to the kind of business that can qualify for as an "S" corp. (for example, an insurance company cannot).*

Failure to meet, or ceasing to meet, these requirements means loss of "S" status and conversion to "C" corp. status-and "C" corp. taxes. These limits and restrictions will be contrasted, below, with the more liberal tax rules for partnerships and LLCs.

"S" corps are often preferred because they are simple to operate. However, they are not suitable for many businesses. The much wider range of options for partnerships and LLCs introduces tax-planning complexity – which may be more than many or most small businesses can effectively use or understand. The use of a tax professional is usually required in determining the appropriate entity to choose.

LLCs and "S" corps share the same business advantage-limitation of liability. "S" corps are a bit better understood by the business community, because LLCs are new and vary from state to state. The tax advantages of LLCs, as compared to "S" corps, are the tax advantages of partnerships. All the points below where LLCs outscore "S" corps arise because LLCs can choose partnership tax status.

*1. LLCs can, to some degree, allocate tax attributes like income or certain kinds of income, depreciation deductions, etc., disproportionately among members to suit their individual tax situations (unlike "S" corps limited by the effect of the single-class-of-stock rule).*

*2. "S" corp. owners can deduct startup or operating losses up to their investment plus any debt that the "S" corp. owes them. LLC members can do the same but can deduct further, up to their share of the debt the LLC owes others.*

*3. Adding co-owners after the entity is formed is easier with LLCs. An outsider's transfer of appreciated property for an LLC membership interest is tax-free. A comparable transfer to an "S" corp. is taxable unless the new co-owner-transferor (or group of transferors) owns more than 80% of the "S" corp. after the transfer.*

*4. Complex tax adjustments ("basis adjustments") can be made by the LLC when LLC interests change hands or LLC property is distributed. These adjustments, unavailable with "S" corps, can have the effect of reducing amounts taxable to certain LLC members.*

*5. Distribution of appreciated LLC property to LLC members is not taxable to the LLC. Comparable "S" corp. distributions to stockholders are taxable to the "S" corp.*

LLCs, with their limited liability for all members, have the edge on general and limited partnerships from a business standpoint. While the federal tax treatment of partners and LLC members is basically the same, there are special tax rules for limited partners (especially self-employment tax rules). It is not clear whether these special tax rules extend to non-manager LLC members. LLCs are more likely than partnerships to be subject to a state tax.

SMLLCs, with their limited liability are preferable for sole proprietors from a business standpoint. Where the sole proprietor so elects, the LLC is ignored and the proprietor is taxed directly under federal tax rules as if no separate entity existed. Some states do, and some do not, ignore the LLC entity for state tax

## 4. CHANGING TO ANOTHER ENTITY:

The many advantages of LLCs, for both business and tax reasons, have encouraged many business owners to convert, or consider converting, to the LLC form. But other changes of entity may suit particular situations – for example, general partnership to LLP (for business reasons) or "C" corp. to "S" corp. (for tax reasons). For tax purposes, a change of entity via a check-the-box decision is treated for tax purposes as an actual change of the entity (whatever may happen under state business law). Here, briefly and in broad outline, is what happens for federal tax purposes when entity status is changed (or treated as changed under check-the-box). How these apply in your own situation must be reviewed in depth with a tax/business advisor.

1. *"C" corp. converts to "S" corp. or vice versa. No tax on the conversion. Pass- through treatment applies while it is an "S" corp.*

2. *"C" corp. or "S" corp. converts to LLC, partnership or sole proprietorship. Generally, a tax on the liquidation of the corporation, with pass-through treatment for the new entity (in modified form in the case of a liquidating "S" corp.).*

3. *Partnership converts to LLC or vice versa; sole proprietorship converts to single member LLC or vice versa. No tax on conversion, pass-through treatment continues.*

4. *LLC, partnership or sole proprietorship converts to "C" or "S" corp. Generally, no tax on conversion. Pass-through treatment (in modified form) for "S" corp. income.*

## CONCLUSION:

While the same state statutes apply to corporations, partnerships and sole proprietorships, the legal aspects of LLCs differ by state and the choice of entity for tax purpose may differ from the legal aspects. Accordingly, while the LLC may provide greater benefit, both the state requirements and the tax requirements are considerations that require the assistance of a professional knowledgeable on both.

## About Richard

Richard B. Soscia, MBA, CFP, DABFA, president of Summit Financial Services Group, is considered a Strategic Thinker and a well-known leader in Entrepreneurship, Business Operations, Accounting, Finance, Economics, and Manufacturing and Business Intelligence. Richard's consultative and leadership experience spans a wide variety of business types and sizes. A clear and consistent record of success in financial planning initiatives, project management, developing effective business models and strategies, and providing insolvency and restructuring advice, serves as a testament to Richard's strategic way of thinking. This standard of excellence has come to define Richard's passion and effectiveness in helping his clients achieve both personal and corporate success.

Richard is a recognized expert on a variety of accounting, business management and taxation issues. His experience in public speaking includes a vast array of business, finance, tax and economic topics. He also serves as an associate professor, mentor and an adjunct professor in colleges and universities in New York – on subjects such as accounting, tax, finance and MBA curricula.

Currently, Richard leads his own successful accounting and consulting group as its President, in which his experience and knowledge have helped him achieve personal and business financial success. To learn more about Richard B. Soscia, MBA, CFP, DABFA, visit: www.summitfinservices.com and to receive your three special business guidance reports emphasizing the positive aspects of business:

1. *CREATING BUSINESS VALUE*

2. *10 STEPS TO SMALL BUSINESS SUCCESS and*

3. *KEEP CUSTOMERS HAPPY,*

Contact Info:
e-mail him at: clients.summit@att.net or call 845-427-7017.

# CHAPTER 3

# Tax Savings For Home-based Businesses

## By Michael Murray, CPA, MBA

What would you say if I told you that a home-based business might generate deductions for you equivalent to about $100 per hour? Well, it's true. Done right, a home-based business is the best tax-planning opportunity in the tax code.

Warning! I strongly advise that no one should ever start a home-based business for the purpose of getting tax deductions only. Businesses just don't work that way. According to tax law businesses must have a profit-seeking motive. This means the business must be out to make money, not just save taxes. Tax deductions are a result of operating a home-based business, definitely not the reason for starting a business. A part-time home-based business may be that idea you just wanted to try, a safety net for your job, the "extra income" for something special or maybe a way out of a less than fulfilling job. Whatever your reason for starting a business, the tax advantages may help you get it started and make it just a bit more worthwhile. So what are the issues and what kind of expenses can the home-based business deduct?

First, a business must establish that it is formed for a "profit motive". When most businesses start up they need to develop a business plan showing that the idea behind the business provides a path to profit. This is not one of those fancy, hundred-page, chart-filled documents, just a summary of the idea and what it will take to make the business profitable. Businesses operate on a regular and consistent basis. This does not mean forty hours a week; as little as three hours a week has been held to be adequate for some businesses. And last, run the business like a business. This means keeping good records, maintaining bank and credit card accounts separate from personal accounts, seeking professional help when appropriate, and doing what can be done to constantly improve your business. Got the idea?

The IRS looks at nine basic factors when evaluating the profit motive of a business, but for the home-based business, the key ones are:

*1. Does the time and effort put into the activity indicate an intention to make a profit? This is where records of regular and consistent operation of the business provide the evidence you need to counter the IRS. The IRS audit guide suggests that reports be available to monitor the business at least quarterly.*

*2. Does the taxpayer depend on the income from the activity? You don't have to be making a full time income to say your family "depends" on the income you make, and as you'll see, the tax benefits could also be something you depend on.*

*3. Are losses due to circumstances beyond the control of the taxpayer or during the startup? It's not unusual to have losses as you start up a business, and businesses often spend money to grow. Also, sometimes an unusual circumstance causes losses. There is no profit in three out of five year "rule" – that's just a guideline that can presume you are a business organized for profit.*

*4. If there are losses, has the taxpayer changed methods of operation to improve profitability? Did you seek professional help, training, or do other things any business would do to improve its outlook? If so, you've indicated a profit motive.*

*5. Does the taxpayer or his/her advisors have the knowledge needed to carry on the activity as a successful business? Again, training and experience are the keys to showing that you know something about the business. Many small businesses have been created by individuals turning a hobby, special interest or passion, into a business.*

What can you deduct if you're operating a home-based business? Section 162 of the Internal Revenue Code says, "There shall be allowed as a deduction all the ordinary and necessary expenses paid or incurred during the taxable year in carrying on any trade or business..." While there are certainly many other rules when it comes to business expenses, this is the basic one. If the expense is necessary for your business and hasn't been specifically excluded by law, it's deductible. Let's take a look at some of the big ones!

When you set up an office in your home and use it exclusively for your business, you may deduct a portion of your utility bills, maintenance, insurance, and even depreciation on the house. Congress made it clear to the IRS that this was an acceptable deduction by changing the rules when the IRS targeted this deduction for audit in the 1990's. Your office may be any "visually identifiable space" under current law. So, the desk and area around it in the one room apartment is an office. There are some rules for the calculations and more than a few tricks to the amounts you may deduct but none of these expenses are deductible without a home-based business. To document your use of property, you must keep records of how much time you spent using it for business and using it for other purposes. This rule applies to your home office and "listed property," items that the IRS believes people often use for personal purposes, including autos, computers and cameras. When you keep track of the time you spend in your home office, you "prove" that you use it regularly and you work regularly. You can keep these records in a log, journal or appointment book. Though it depends on many factors, your home office deduction can easily amount to more than $1,000 per year.

The tax code allows a standard mileage allowance, 55.5 cents per mile as of 7/1/2011, so for every business mile you drive there's a deduction. When you take care of a personal errand while on a business trip, the stop at the grocery store is deductible. Anytime you leave your home office and drive for a necessary business purpose, such as a business appointment, training or meeting, you can take a deduction. This deduction requires keeping a log of miles and the purpose of the trip. This is really simple documentation for such a large deduction, in fact there's an app for that. If you drive an average of about 100 business miles per week, you would get a $2,900 per year deduction.

Any meals and entertainment related to the business are 50% deductible. There are several rules here but if it is ordinary and necessary to carrying on your business, it's deductible. Ordinary and necessary in this context usually means that you expect a business benefit, you talk about things that further that business benefit, the reason for the entertainment is business and the person you fed or entertained could help produce the benefit. Documenting business-entertainment expenses is not difficult, but the rules are strict. Date, amount, place, purpose and person must be recorded contemporaneously. Because most people don't know the rules and because the record-keeping requirements are somewhat technical, it's easy for the IRS auditors to "catch" taxpayers with inadequate records. Just because meals and entertainment expenses are frequently reviewed in audits, is no reason to ignore these deductions on your tax return. As long as you document the expenses properly, you can let the IRS audit all they like – you've got the proof. I suggest using an expense app on your Smartphone to make receipt keeping and documentation quick, easy and contemporaneous. When done correctly, your golfing or other activity is a business expense.

Meals and entertainment can easily add $1,000 or more in deductions you would not otherwise get.

Salaries paid for necessary activities in your business are deductible. Why not pay your children to do some of the filing and other clerical tasks. Children as young as six years old can qualify as employees of their parents' sole proprietorship and are not subject to social security, medicare or unemployment taxes. Also the first $5,700 your child earns is not subject to income tax and the next $8,500 is only taxed at a 10% rate. This deduction may provide the greatest single planning opportunity of all. Imagine your child being able to pay for dance lessons, swim club and summer camp with pretax dollars from his or her own account. Documenting what your employees do and its relationship to your business is as easy as keeping a log of when the children work. One child's wages could easily be a $5,700 deduction or more and you still get the dependency deduction you've always gotten.

Most taxpayers never get to deduct unreimbursed medical expenses since they never rise above 7.5% of adjusted gross income. Large corporations offer flexible spending arrangements within cafeteria plans to help their employees. As a small business owner you can hire your spouse and provide a medical expense reimbursement plan. You will want to get some help here because you'll need W-2's and other reporting requirements for the IRS and state. Despite these hurdles, the benefits more than make up for the administrative costs. These plans allow all unreimbursed medical expenses and insurance premiums to be deducted as employee benefits rather than medical expenses. A plan document, some receipts and a bit of administration, and the deduction is yours. Even with your employer's health insurance, this can easily amount to $1,000 or more per year and if you're not covered by your employer, – then your insurance also becomes an employee benefit.

Speaking of employee benefits, your employees, spouse and children can also be part of your retirement plan to shelter even more of your hard-earned money from taxes. Imagine being able to provide a retirement plan for your children before they reach middle school. This is also a great way to help you make up for some of those years of missed contributions to your employer-sponsored retirement plan. Retirement plans are complex and require plan documents and very strict observance of the rules, but the savings can be really substantial.

A home-based business also provides the perfect way to deduct nearly all of your vacations as a business expense as well. Most businesses can find a convention, show or training function at a desirable resort. As long as the function is the primary purpose of the trip and more than half the days were business days, the trip is deductible. The law has some taxpayer-friendly definitions of business days which make this better than you may think. Business days include travel days, weekends and holidays between business days, any day with four or more hours of business activities and any day with a prescheduled business appointment. So with a bit of planning, the family vacation becomes a business trip. You'll deduct at least $2,500 per year and enjoy it!

If you've been keeping a running total, that's $14,100 or more, plus retirement benefits, in deductions that your investment of 156 hours per year could be getting you. Even if you can't take advantage of all those deductions, you can see why I said $100 per hour is a realistic expectation. $100 per hour is $208,000 per year in a regular job. That's what the top three percent, 3 out of every 100, of all taxpayers earned in 2008 according to IRS information. Are you among that elite group? Couldn't you find a few hours per week in your schedule to get your home-based business benefitting you and your family?

One last thought, since unincorporated small businesses seem to be selected for audit a bit more frequently than the average tax return, I suggest that you find a CPA who is very familiar with home-based businesses. This is a specialty area of tax law just like employment taxes or gift and estate taxes. In the audit environment, the IRS doesn't take your word for anything. You'll have to come up with receipts, cancelled checks, bank statements, and other records to support both the amount of income you claimed and any business deductions you took. You really can throw it all in a shoebox if you want, but most business owners find it easier to keep receipts filed as they go. To document income, you'll need copies of your bank statements, copies of checks you've deposited, copies of any 1099s you received, and, if you have non-taxable income, copies of documents showing the source of that income – for example, income from an inheritance.

Remember, the IRS is less interested in the business income you reported than in the income it thinks you failed to report. This means your job is not really to prove the amount of income your business earned, but to prove that any deposits to your accounts you didn't report as income came from a nontaxable source. To document most business expenses, you must keep records showing what you bought, who you bought it from, how much you paid, and the date of the purchase. In most cases, you can prove this with your receipt and a cancelled check or credit card statement, which proves that the receipt is really yours. Those who specialize in home-based businesses can guide you in the documentation and taxation issues of your business so that should you be audited, you'll get through it with ease.

CPA's who specialize in home-based businesses often have services geared to the home-based business market that help with the record-keeping, and keep you on top of the ever-changing tax code. These specialists bridge the gap between accounting and bookkeeping. Accounting is the process of managing and forecasting financial affairs. An accountant prepares financial reports and tax returns to advise the business owner. Bookkeeping, on the other hand, is a subset of the accounting activity, where information is compiled and accounts are kept up-to-date. If you want to do it yourself, I'd recommend one of the accounting programs like QuickBooks or a customized software accounting solution created for your specific business. Keep the supporting documents like receipts and statements for your entries. But remember, you should use a good accountant to tie it all together.

A good CPA can also help you select an appropriate opportunity for your needs. I recommend opportunities that provide residual income from multiple products that you feel good about. Small businesses survive largely on the owner's passion and dreams. I have clients who are in all stages of their home-based businesses. Some who start a home-based business as a part time venture develop a full-time profitable business and take control of their personal, financial, business and tax life. Others remain happily making a little and saving taxes in their part-time business.

Knowing that the tax code can help your home-based business just may make it easier to get started.

## About Michael

Michael G. Murray, CPA, MBA provides accounting, tax, and consulting services to his individual and small business clients. With a specialty in home-based businesses, he provides done-for-you accounting and tax planning. He has over 40 years of experience in accounting and consulting. Mike networks with many business relationships in the banking, legal and insurance areas to help his clients grow their businesses. A creative problem solver, Mike is frequently asked to assist his clients in trouble-shooting business challenges.

Mike founded Murray CPA in October 1988. Prior to starting Murray CPA, Mike held positions as accountant and consultant at a small firm and at a large international firm, a CFO at a restaurant chain, and also held various positions at a major distribution company.

Mike received his Bachelor of Business Administration degree in Accounting from the University of Wisconsin, and his Masters in Business Administration from Lake Forest Graduate School of Management. Mike earned his CPA designation in January 1971. He has a passion for his family, clients, sports, music, and travel.

Contact information:
www.accountantlibertyville.com
www.mgmcpa.com

# CHAPTER 4

# What to Do When the IRS Comes Calling

## By E. Dennis Bridges, CPA

**W**ithout a doubt, the IRS is everybody's favorite government agency to hate. The very thought of getting even a single letter from the IRS makes most people break out in a cold sweat. The over-riding purpose of this chapter is to show that there is a light at the end of the tunnel in dealing with the IRS, and that – surprisingly – the IRS can be approachable in reaching a livable solution to most prior-year tax problems.

To illustrate this, we'll give some real life examples – cases that we have actually had in our office – along with real-life solutions. In the process, we'll try to provide a sense of what drives us to help taxpayers this way – what gives us our passion. If you or someone you know are nagged with either a minor or serious IRS issue, our goal is to help you sleep tonight knowing that there are options for your specific situation.

In the course of resolving IRS problems for taxpayers, particularly in more serious cases, clients frequently ask us any of several questions like:

- *How is it that we deal with the IRS on a daily basis when most people live in fear of them?*

- *How did we get started with assisting taxpayers this way?*
- *Where do we get our drive for what we do?*

While tax problem resolution is not the only area that we concentrate in, it is the segment of our practice where we truly connect with taxpayers, almost like a major league ball player connecting with a fastball and sending it into the left-field seats.

To explain what I mean by "connecting," let me give you a real-life example right out of my own family. My wife Robin, and I, are blessed with two daughters, Katherine and Kimberly. Katherine is "wired" much more like Robin in the way she thinks and learns. Sadly for Kimberly, she is wired much more like me. Some 15 years ago, when Kimberly was in grade school, she was having a tough time learning how to make and count change. Robin had tried unsuccessfully several times to teach Kimberly, and both were becoming very frustrated. After all, Katherine, our older daughter, had learned it with little difficulty.

Robin told me about her frustration (and Kimberly's). In one of my precious few fits of genius, I went down into our basement, set up a table, and created "Dad's General Store". I brought down a whole box full of items to "sell", including pencils, erasers, a couple of dolls and a stuffed animal or two.

First, Kimberly "shopped" and I was the shopkeeper, carefully counting out the change to her for each of her individual purchases. Then we switched places, and a miracle happened right then and there. Kimberly's face lit up like a Christmas tree, and she started making change as if she'd always known how – all because we had connected!!

We are driven by the desire to help our clients get from where they are to where they want to be.

Sometimes that consists of helping a taxpayer get out of severe trouble with the IRS. Sometimes it's by cutting someone's tax debt from $100,000 down to $13,000.

Tax law can sometimes be a daunting subject for even the most 'seasoned' attorney or CPA. For that reason, I'm going to try to keep our discussion as non-technical as possible. The guidance that I want to provide for you is less about giving you the specific solution for your situation than it is to provide a measure of hope for you in knowing that there are numerous options available, regardless of your circumstances.

In the realm of tax litigation and IRS problem resolution, there is little that we haven't seen.

We deal with relatively minor situations that can be "fixed" in a day. And we also deal with very severe situations that may require months before we find or negotiate the desired outcome, or at least an acceptable one.

This chapter is not about me, or about our practice. It's about you, and how you can make the very best of an unpleasant tax situation. However, if you've made it this far in this chapter, you deserve to know just a bit about my background.

I've had the privilege of being mentored throughout my career by two of the foremost authorities in the country in the area of IRS practice. One is Robert Shreibman, a tax attorney from Torrance, California just outside Los Angeles. He had a very gracious secretary years ago, Jane Subeck, who told me that he had taken a special interest in me and in "bringing me along." I suspect the truth was more that he just felt sorry for me with the sometimes constant questions with which I would nag him back in the early days. Mr. Shreibman has been a law school professor, author, speaker, and defender in numerous high profile cases over the years.

The other is Jim Wilson, a practitioner and lecturer out of Indianapolis, a man of true wisdom and brilliance. A few years ago, I had the opportunity of speaking at a conference of about 200 attorneys and CPAs in Denver. In the middle of my presentation, I glanced out into the audience, and there was Jim Wilson about ten rows back. He should have been the speaker and I the listener.

With that introduction, I want to pass along to you just five simple principles that guide us in seeking relief for taxpayers throughout the country. These same principles can guide you in reaching a livable solution to your IRS problem(s):

## 1. Don't Wait 'til the Last Minute.

Let's face it – we're all human and we tend to put off the stuff that's unpleasant. The only problem is, in dealing with the IRS, the longer you wait to deal with your matter, the more unpleasant it will be. If you're over 40, you may remember the Fram Oil Filter commercial from years ago where the mechanic says, "Pay me now, or…pay me later." The clear message is, you can pay a small price now to keep your engine in good shape, or you can pay a big price later on. The same rule applies to dealing with the IRS. Sadly, we had a case where our client had procrastinated to the point where the IRS showed up at his house with sheriff's deputies and a moving truck fully prepared to conduct a seizure of property. There was no need for their tax problems to ever go that far downhill.

We were able to get the seizure halted and worked out an arrangement acceptable to both sides. The Agent in charge, an acquaintance of mine, told me later that she actually felt sorry for the husband – because it was very clear from the moment the IRS and deputies arrived, that the husband was in much more trouble with his wife than with the IRS.

## 2. Be Prepared!

One of the most common solutions to deal with a prior-year IRS problem is a monthly installment agreement. While there are several different types of agreements, the most common is a standard agreement where the taxpayer enters into an arrangement to pay the IRS an amount roughly equal to the household discretionary income, i.e., "bring-home pay" less reasonable household expenses. Whether you choose to deal with the IRS directly or retain a professional to represent you, you will come out well ahead by having a good fix on your monthly income and expense picture.

### 3. Everything is Negotiable (...Well, almost)

Part of what scares people about dealing with the IRS is their seeming authority to make people owe money out of thin air. The following three examples will hopefully give taxpayers a bit of comfort that liabilities of different kinds can be reduced:

*a.* ***Audits*** - If you've been through a tax audit, even if it's already "closed," you have the right to appeal the IRS' proposed adjustments or re-open the case with a process known as audit reconsideration. We've represented taxpayers in numerous cases throughout the country where we didn't even prepare the original returns, and were able to reach a more pleasant result by either re-constructing records or pointing out an error on the part of the examiner.

*b.* ***Collections cases*** – If you owe prior-year balances to the IRS, whether for income tax or payroll taxes, the IRS is more negotiable than ever. For the first time in modern history, the IRS is being run by an individual from the world of private enterprise, i.e., a past business owner, rather than a career government employee. And guess what – he's actually starting to run the IRS like a business! For example, the IRS will now allow what we call a stair-step installment agreement, where the IRS agrees to accept a lower monthly payment initially, in order to allow time for the taxpayer to get his or her finances in order.

*c.* ***Amended Returns*** – Many taxpayers are already aware that prior-year returns can be amended for a couple of years. Actually, previous tax returns can be amended for any year where there is still an open balance. (The taxpayer that I mentioned earlier where we were able to reduce their balance from $100,000 down to $13,000, we did largely by amending his returns over a six-year period for business expenses that had been overlooked by his original preparer.)

## 4. Choose the right representative

If you are seeking professional representation to assist in the resolution of your tax matter, choose carefully. Most importantly, find a firm or individual that knows their stuff, but also someone you can connect with. If the IRS has filed a Federal Tax Lien against you, you have probably started getting a mailbox full of solicitations from firms all over the country disguised as official mail or coming from the IRS. If possible, ask for a referral from either your accountant or attorney. If nothing else, call at least three or four firms and compare them. Regardless of what you do for a living, you are not a cow and you shouldn't feel like a number or like you are being herded through a "one-size-fits-all" process.

If your funds are severely limited and you are simply unable to pay for professional guidance, contact the IRS' Taxpayer Advocate Office in your area. While they are indeed a part of the IRS, they have a degree of independence and one of their purposes is to deal with hardship cases. If your current situation is severe enough that you are considering bankruptcy, do yourself a favor and seek out a bankruptcy attorney that is experienced in dealing with IRS issues in bankruptcy. There are actually instances where income taxes may be dischargeable (wiped out) in the bankruptcy process. [Section 507(a) and 523(a) of the U.S. Bankruptcy Code deal with the conditions under which income taxes are dischargeable.] Again, check with your attorney.

## 5. Remember "The Golden Rule"

You know, the one that says, "Treat other people the way you'd want to be treated yourself".

I realize this is easier said than done, particularly when you know that the person on the phone (or on your front porch) is trying to take money from you that you'd much rather spend on fun or family. Believe it or not, the IRS is approachable, particularly if you can try to be civil during your phone call or personal contact with them.

In our office we have IRS conferences at least three days a week. With each call or contact, we start off with a desired result. I can tell you without fear of error that our pleasant demeanor has been our "secret weapon" in many borderline cases or issues.

At the same time, I appreciate the honesty of many taxpayers who call saying they would feel much better entrusting their IRS problem to us, even if it was relatively minor. If you should find yourself on the phone with the IRS and you either feel that you're getting "railroaded" or simply don't sense that things are going in a comfortable direction, simply ask the representative for his or her name and badge number, and tell the representative that you'd like to call back at another time.

The IRS has also become more negotiable in the options that are available and in flexibility with those options. Doubtless you have heard of one of their popular options known as an "Offer in Compromise." This is a negotiated settlement with the desired result of the IRS agreeing to settle for hopefully a substantially lower amount than what is owed. While this option is still available, we rarely use it simply because there are other options that are far superior and yield a significantly better result, very often at a significantly lower cost to the taxpayer.

Part of the reward for us in assisting taxpayers in resolving IRS issues is in the process of determining the very best result for a given situation, and even in creating a "Plan B" just in case.

As I said earlier in the chapter, we are driven by the desire to help our clients get from where they are to where they want to be. If we can help a family or a business out of a severe situation with the IRS, help them get into compliance and even show them how to legally lower their taxes for the future, then we've done our job and achieved our mission.

## About Dennis

Dennis Bridges is a CPA and a leading authority in the favorable resolution of serious IRS difficulties. He has practiced in the Atlanta area for over 25 years, and assists individuals and businesses throughout the country in solving severe income and payroll tax issues.

He is a frequent speaker and the author of numerous articles and two other books: *On Level Ground With The IRS* and *The Ultimate Tax Relief Toolkit*. He is available for speaking engagements and private consultations, schedule permitting.

For a limited time, he will give a free 30-minute consultation to readers of *Breaking The Tax Code*. He can be reached at 770-984-8008, or through his website: edbcpa.com

# CHAPTER 5

# Tax Benefits Of Retirement Planning

## By Jeffrey L. Upchurch, CPA

If you're working, chances are your company offers some sort of retirement plan, the most popular being the 401(k). A 401(k) plan offers the employee the opportunity to contribute pre-tax earnings to the retirement plan and none of the earnings/contributions will be counted as taxable income to the employee. Plus, many employers will match a portion of the amount contributed by the employee, which is essentially free money.

My clients often ask me how they can reduce their taxes. My response to many of them is to ask what they are doing to save for retirement. The U.S. tax code is written to encourage saving for retirement, but penalizes you for withdrawing from retirement accounts before you reach retirement age.

For example, assume you make $100,000 per year, which puts you in the 28% tax bracket. If you contribute 10% of your salary to your 401(k) plan, your taxes would be reduced by $2,800 ($10,000 x 28%). For 2011, the IRS will allow you to contribute a maximum of $16,500 to a 401(k), which in this example, would reduce your tax liability by more than $4,600.

For those closer to retirement age, there are even more benefits because the IRS allows a "catch-up" contribution of an additional $5,500. You have to be at least 50 years old to take advantage of this option, though.

Using the same example from above, but assuming you max out your 401(k) contribution of $16,500, and you're over 50. You're able to contribute an additional $5,500 towards retirement, for a total of $22,000 contributed to your account this year. In addition to setting aside money for retirement, you've reduced your taxable income to $78,000, which changed your upper tax bracket from 28% to 25%, and reduced your tax bill by almost $6,750.

If you're not currently contributing to your 401(k) plan, it's never too late to start. I recently started working with a client Gerri, who was in this exact situation. Gerri was a schoolteacher for 35 years, but she retired about 5 years ago and has been collecting her pension since. She was bored in retirement, though, so she went back to work as an education consultant. Counting her pension and wages from her current job, Gerri earns more than $100,000 per year. After talking to Gerri about her income taxes, we discovered that her current company offered a 401(k) but she wasn't contributing to it. She didn't think she needed to because she thought she had enough money for retirement. It turns out Gerri's pension provides her more than enough money to live on, and she didn't really need the income from her current job to survive, so I advised her to contribute the maximum allowed plus the catch up contribution to her 401(k) in the current year. She was a little hesitant until I explained how much money she would be saving in taxes.

This story is great to hear if you're in a similar situation to Gerri, but what if you're 23 years old just starting your career? The 401(k) is still a great option for you and I highly recommend taking advantage of it if it's offered by your employer. However, there is a relatively new retirement plan being offered that is perfect for those with many years until retirement. I'm talking about the ROTH 401(k). This is different to a "regular" 401(k) plan because money contributed to a ROTH 401(k) is part of your taxable income or "after tax" dollars.

So what's the tax benefit? All earnings from a ROTH 401(k) are completely tax free. Using the same example as before, but assuming you contributed $10,000 to a ROTH 401(k) plan, your taxable income for the current year remains $100,000 and you'll be paying taxes on the amount contributed. However, the $10,000 you contributed grows tax-free. Similar to a regular 401(k), you can't withdraw funds from your ROTH 401(k) account until you are 59.5 years old, but you won't pay income taxes on any withdrawals because you have already paid taxes on the original contribution.

If you expect tax rates to be higher when you retire than they are now, are a high income earner, or are a relatively new taxpayer, then a ROTH 401(k) plan might be the right option for you.

There are even more retirement options outside of your job that may reduce your tax liability — such as an IRA or ROTH IRA. You're allowed to contribute up to $5,000 towards your IRA or ROTH IRA each year, and contributions to your IRA may be deductible on your tax return. This amount increases to $6,000 if you're 50 years old or over. Whether you can take the deduction or not depends on a number of circumstances including your income and whether you or your spouse's employer offers a retirement plan, so please consult your tax advisor regarding your specific circumstances.

The maximum contribution amounts above are further limited by your current year wages. For example, I have a client, who coincidentally is also a retired schoolteacher, who contributes to her IRA every year. She occasionally works as a substitute teacher and only earns about $2,000 per year doing this. The maximum amount she's allowed to contribute to her IRA is equal to her earnings of $2,000 each year. But if she didn't make this contribution she'd pay approximately $500 more in taxes every year.

The ROTH IRA works similar to a ROTH 401(k) in that contributions to this type of plan do not reduce your tax liability in the year of the contribution, but all earnings from a ROTH IRA are tax free. There are income limitations on who can contribute to a ROTH IRA, but it's a fantastic option for those allowed to participate.

If you own a business, there are even better retirement plan options, which can result in significantly greater tax savings. The SEP IRA is the most common retirement plan used by small business owners, but they may also utilize a 401(k), ROTH 401(k), Pension or other plans specifically designed for small businesses. Your choice of plan will depend upon your goals and overall objective.

Payments to the retirement plan will be either business expenses or personal tax deductions.

A few years ago I picked up a new client who I'll call Brian. Brian was in his mid-thirties and the owner of a very profitable small business, earning about $200,000 each year after expenses. Prior to becoming a client of mine, he usually contributed $49,000 to his SEP IRA annually, which is the maximum allowed. Over a period of several years, his retirement account had accumulated to approximately $500,000, and he had limited his tax liability by approximately $10,000 each year because of the contribution.

When I first met with Brian, we started talking about his long-term financial plans. He said he was more concerned with saving for retirement, and wanted to continue maximizing the amount contributed according to the law. Brian also said that saving was more important to him than lowering his tax liability each year. Most people I meet with just want to reduce their tax liability as much as they can, and any retirement savings accumulated during that time are a bonus. With that in mind, I started discussing different retirement options with Brian and the tax implications of each. We discussed how the maximum he's allowed to contribute is $49,000 each year, and there is nothing we can do to increase that amount. However, utilizing different types of retirement plans will result in a different tax liability now, and potentially in the future.

Brian was particularly interested in the Roth 401(k) plan. The maximum he's allowed to contribute to this type of plan is $16,500 per year, and he understood that contributions made to a Roth 401(k) are included in his taxable income, resulting in a higher tax liability this year. But it also meant he would not be taxed on any withdrawals from this plan when he retired. Because his primary goal was to save for retirement, this type of plan made the most sense for Brian. He would pay a little more in taxes now, but assuming his retirement account grew in value, he would pay less in taxes in future years. Under this scenario, Brian would then contribute $32,500 to his SEP IRA account, thereby maximizing his allowable contributions.

And there are more options for Brian too. Because his contributions to the ROTH 401(k) are included in his taxable income, his tax liability is approximately $4,000 higher than in prior years. If Brian was to change his mind and wanted his tax liability to increase by only $2,000, he could reduce his contributions to the ROTH 401(k) from the maximum of $16,500 to $8,250. He could then contribute $40,650 to his SEP IRA account or his company could match his ROTH 401(k) contribution into a regular 401(k) account and the difference under $49,000 could be contributed to his SEP IRA account. Either way, Brian still saves a total of $49,000 for retirement. The only difference between these scenarios is whether the retirement plan contributions are made with pre or post tax dollars and whether the contributions are tax deductible.

In the end Brian decided to maximize his contribution to the Roth 401(k) account with the remainder amount allowed contributed to his SEP IRA account. But how do you know which retirement option is right for you? Unfortunately there is no one-size-fits-all answer.

If you work for a corporation that offers a 401(k) or similar retirement plan, there are usually advisors to assist you through the enrollment and setup process. However, I also recommend working with an independent financial advisor and a qualified tax professional. The financial advisor can help you allocate your investments in your 401(k) plan, and working together, the two professionals will assist you develop a tax and retirement plan strategy. This may include contributing to an IRA or ROTH IRA account, depending on your particular circumstances.

These professionals can also identify certain options in your company's retirement plan of which you weren't aware. For example, many 401(k) plans will not allow you to transfer your account assets to a different retirement plan (such as a personal IRA) while still employed with the sponsoring company. However it's becoming more common for 401(k) plans to offer "in-service" transfers. This option allows you to transfer your 401(k) assets to a different retirement plan, such as your personal IRA, while you're still employed with your company. On the surface, this option might not seem like a big deal. But if your 401(k) has poor or a limited number of investment options, this is a great option. Further, if your company's 401(k) is changing plan administrators, it's likely your account will be frozen for 60-90 days.

During this time you won't be able to make any investment changes or withdrawals from your account. Again, you might wonder why that's such a big deal. But remember that is exactly what happened to the employees of Enron as it was collapsing. While the company stock was tumbling lower and lower with each passing day, their accounts were frozen and they couldn't sell their company stock. By the time the accounts were unfrozen, their Enron investments were virtually worthless.

Similarly, business owners need to select qualified tax and financial advisors. The regulations are extremely complicated, but the stakes are even higher. Using Brian's example above, if he were to contribute more than $49,000 per year or do something else not allowed under tax law, the IRS could cancel the retirement plan entirely. As a result, all the assets of the plan would be taxable income to Brian.

The key points to remember are there are several tax benefits to saving for retirement, but the laws and regulations are complicated, and you should always consult your tax and financial advisors to discuss your specific tax and retirement tax plan.

## About JEFFREY

Jeffrey L. Upchurch is a Certified Public Accountant who has worked on major corporate, nonprofit and healthcare financial issues; lectured in university, medical and nonprofit settings; and been involved in numerous civic and volunteer efforts. He is a specialist in IRS-problem resolution and other tax-related topics.

Upchurch holds a Bachelor of Science degree in Accounting from Bradley University in Peoria, Ill. He graduated in 2000 and passed the CPA exam the first time he sat for it. He proudly points out that only about 15 percent of people taking that exam accomplish such a feat.

Prior to starting his own accounting firm, Upchurch worked for more than five years at Deloitte & Touche LLP, one of the largest CPA firms in the world. For over two years, he also worked for Northwestern Memorial Hospital, a top Chicago medical center affiliated with Northwestern University.

Jeff started his own accounting business, Upchurch & Associates, in 2009. Based in Chicago's NorthCenter neighborhood, an established area experiencing a youthful revival, this accounting firm focuses on the needs of individuals, nonprofit organizations and small businesses. Upchurch also has been a guest lecturer in Chicago at DePaul University, the Pacific College of Oriental Medicine, and the Center for Nonprofit Success, as part of its leadership series.

Jeff, his wife, their new daughter and adopted dog, Barnie, live in the NorthCenter area. He is active throughout the north side of Chicago: volunteering at the Neighborhood Boys and Girls Club of Chicago carnival and the NorthCenter Chamber of Commerce "Ribfest," participating in networking groups such as LeTip of Lakeview, and formerly serving on the board of directors of the Albany Park Community Center.

For more information about Jeffrey L. Upchurch, or to arrange an interview or speaking engagement, please call: (773) 360-8280 or write to: info@chicago-accountant.com.

# CHAPTER 6

# "I Can Deduct THAT?"

## By Jon Neal, CPA, MST, PFS

I don't know how many times I have heard that question when meeting with a client. Normally, it is with a new client as we review their prior year tax returns. With all the deductions available, it is no wonder. Every year, 'heck,' every day, the rules change. Something that was deductible is not now or it is only under certain situations. Something that was not deductible is now deductible. The IRS devotes entire publications to a single deduction. Reading these publications often leaves you more confused than before you started. Often, we save clients thousands of dollars by asking the right questions about their personal and financial lives.

Meet Joe. He is a single guy who is a construction worker and travels all over the state. He uses his own vehicle to travel. When I met with Joe, he thought he had a "simple" return. "I just take the standard deduction since I rent and don't have any kids" he told me. When I asked him about his job he told me his story. "Do you get reimbursed for your mileage?" I asked him. "My employer pays me $400 a month for a car allowance." I asked to see a paystub. Looking at it, I told Joe that the car allowance was included in his W-2 income. "How many miles do you put on your vehicle?" I asked. After he told me, we ended up amending his last three years tax returns and getting Joe a nice-sized refund of over $1,700.

Meet Karen and Alex. They came in to see me because they had sold some investments, and in doing their own taxes thought were going to owe a lot of money. Karen called me and asked if I would look at their information. Of course I would! They had put $1,000 into some mutual funds when they first got married and now were selling some to buy a house. They received about $20,000 and thought they would owe about $5,000 to the IRS. I asked them some questions and found that they had reinvested their dividends over the years. Thankfully, Karen had kept good records. I explained that those reinvested dividends could be added to their original investment and reduce the gain they would have to pay taxes on. When we "crunched" the numbers, they ended up with a small loss due to the stock market fluctuations. They certainly left my office with smiles on their faces!

## Here are twelve other deductions that are often missed:

*1. Volunteer mileage* – You can deduct a cents-per-mile amount established by the IRS for volunteer work. Say you serve meals to the homeless with your church every week. It is 20 miles round trip from your church to the serving place. That can mean a few more dollars in your pocket at tax time.

*2. Medical mileage* – Driving to the doctor, dentist or hospital is deductible. You must be above the overall limitation on medical expenses to claim the deduction and sometimes this nudges you over the minimum amount.

*3. Expenses paid for charity* – Every Christmas season our church has what they call a "Circle of Love." Others may call it a "Giving Tree" or "Sharing the Season." The point is, what you buy as gifts and contribute to that organization is tax deductible. Remember to keep your receipts, credit card receipt or copy of the check. The same holds true for items you buy for food drives, clothing drives or natural disaster special collections.

*4. Non-financial donations* – I refer to this as "stuff" versus "cash." Many people have the wrong impression that they can only deduct up to $500 of clothes, toys, sports equipment and the like given to Goodwill, Salvation Army, Hadassah, St. Vincent DePaul or similar organizations. Not true. Keep good lists of what you donate, possibly even take pictures. Attach the receipt from the organization to that list. You can determine the value of your donations from thrift shops or rummage sales.

**5. *Points paid on the purchase or refinancing of a home*** – If you pay "points" when you buy a new personal residence they are deductible in full in the year of purchase. Points may also be called loan origination fees, commitment fees or loan discount fees. If they are based on a percentage of the mortgage they are deductible. When you refinance your mortgage the points cannot be deducted in full in the year of refinancing. You still get the full deduction but the points must be written off over fifteen years. Many people forget that when they refinance the second (or third, etc.) time, that remaining amount is deducted in full.

**6. *Real estate taxes*** – Most people know that when real estate taxes are paid, they are an itemized deduction. What many overlook is what happens when they sell their residence or second home. The seller is usually credited with "paying" the real estate taxes up to the day of closing. This amount is deductible by the seller on Schedule A.

**7. *Medical expenses*** – Most people know that payments to doctors, dentists and hospitals are deductible as medical expenses. They don't know that glasses and hearing aids are deductible. Also deductible are health insurance premiums paid out of pocket, including Medicare Part B premiums, long-term care premiums, also known as nursing home insurance, alcohol and drug abuse treatment, airfare and lodging expenses for medical travel away from home, and certain improvements or modifications made to your residence for medical reasons.

**8. *State and local income taxes*** – The state and local income taxes withheld from your paychecks are deductible. Many people overlook the estimated tax payments they make to their state and the payment they made this year for last year's amount owed when they filed their taxes. For example, Rick owed the State $630 when he filed his taxes in April this year. When Rick files next year, he can deduct that $630 on Schedule A.

**9. *Advisor fees*** – Payments made to have your taxes professionally prepared are deductible as a miscellaneous deduction on Schedule A. Fees paid to an investment or financial advisor are deductible as well as subscriptions to investment publications or advisory services. Payments to an attorney for tax planning are also deductible. Ask your attorney to separate the cost of preparing a will or power of attorney from the tax planning on the bill you receive.

**10. *Work related expenses*** – Union dues and professional association dues are deductible as miscellaneous deductions. Tools for your trade are deductible. An auto mechanic that has to buy his or her own tools needs to keep good records of the purchases made. There have been many returns I have amended to deduct the tool chest and coveralls a mechanic did not take as a tax deduction. Clothes that cannot be worn by the general public are also deductible. Examples would be safety shoes or clothing with company logos. Sadly, the costs of men's or women's suits and their dry cleaning or laundering are not deductible.

**11. *Self-employed retirement plans*** – I am always amazed when I meet a new client that has a Schedule C for his or her own business. Most of the time there is no deduction for a retirement plan contribution shown on their tax return. When I ask why not, I get two replies: either "I didn't know I could do that" or "I was told it was not worth doing." LISTEN UP! Here is your chance to have the government help pay for your retirement! Every dollar you can deduct saves you taxes. It is an instant return on your investment. Plus, you may qualify for a tax credit for establishing that plan!

How it works is pretty simple. Let's say you are in a 15% tax bracket. That means that for every dollar you earn, the government takes fifteen cents for their pocket. If you put $100 into a retirement account your taxes are reduced by $15. That means the retirement plan only "cost" you $85 after taxes. That doesn't count the actual return your investment will pay you over time.

Why wouldn't you do that, as long as you had the money? I don't know why not either.

*12. Dependents* – This can be a VERY confusing item. In these times, I have decided that nothing will surprise me. Who can you claim as a dependent? The answer is "it depends." First, let's clear up one area. Your spouse is not considered a dependent. Done and done. Now let's talk about your kids. Divorced families, blended families, single parents and traditional families all have their own rules and issues. Is it child support or something else? Who has primary physical custody of the child? What if my child has a child and both live with me? My child is in college and has a good part time job? My child graduated from college and can't find a full time job? Can I still claim my child as a dependent? My advice is to call an expert and ask your questions. Every year the law seems to change so what I tell you today may not be true next year.

What about other dependents? There are more "sandwich families" these days. These are families where your parents are living with you and your children. Can you claim your parents as dependents? What about aunts, uncles, brothers or sisters? Cousins? What if they don't live with you but you pay for their expenses outside of your home? What about your "significant other" that doesn't have a job? Again it is all based on facts and circumstances. Each situation is different and each year the rules may change.

Here's an extra tip! **KEEP GOOD RECORDS!** In real estate they always say it's location, location, location. In taxes, it is **DOCUMENT, DOCUMENT, DOCUMENT!** If you keep good records, two things happen. Actually three. First, when it is time to gather your information for tax preparation you will have everything together and in order. You flip through your records for charitable deductions, add them up and voila! Second, check that off the list and put that number on your tax return. Third, you have the documentation needed if the IRS comes knocking on your door. Remember the words of my wife who is a nurse.

"If you didn't write it down, it didn't happen." She is talking about documenting what happens when taking care of a patient. The same applies to taxes.

In this world we live in, governments are trying to get all the money they can from taxpayers. Recently one of my clients received a letter from the IRS asking for documentation of the medical expenses claimed on their tax return. Fortunately Brian and Janet kept excellent records. We copied everything and sent it in. Awhile later, the IRS sent them a letter saying thank you very much, there is no change. A potentially agonizing situation made easier by having good records. Keep them in a safe, accessible place.

## About Jon

Jon Neal, CPA, MST, PFS has over 34 years of experience in public accounting. In 1977, Jon graduated from the University of Wisconsin-Milwaukee (UWM) with a BBA in Accounting and Management Information Systems, and in 1987 from UWM with a Masters of Science in Taxation (MST). The Neal Group LLC was founded in 1984 after Jon decided to leave as partner of a large, local CPA firm.

He is especially focused on closely-held businesses and their owners, to help them reach their goals. Jon has helped hundreds of businesses grow by offering hands-on assistance in accounting systems, business creation and expansion, tax planning, financial planning, organizational development and acquisition strategies. In 2007, Jon received the Personal Financial Specialist (PFS) designation from the American Institute of Certified Public Accountants to reflect the years spent with clients planning for their retirement, family protection and succession planning.

Jon received his CPA license in 1980 and is a member of the AICPA and WICPA. Jon also carries Series 7, 63 and 66 securities licenses. Milwaukee Magazine has named Jon a Five Star Wealth Advisor in the accounting area for 2009, 2010 and 2011. He is only one of three CPA's in the Milwaukee Area to be so honored. Jon is the author of The Best Doggone Tax Advice, has appeared on various television shows and had a radio show since 2010 called "The Best Doggone Tax and Financial Advice."

Personally, Jon enjoys singing in his church's choir, spending time with his family, his dog and doing volunteer work. Jon and his wife, Ann, have four children and live in Hales Corners.

## CHAPTER 7

# Retiring Without The IRS:
## *The Secret of Making Your Golden Years Less Taxing*

By Mark MacDonald

*"You can be young without money
but you can't be old without it."*
~Tennessee Williams

What if I told you almost everything you know about saving for retirement might be wrong!

That may sound like a strong statement, but there are a great many facts to back it up. 72% of all working Americans approaching retirement age are planning on a 401(k) and/or IRA to help fund their retirement income. Many of them believe their 401(k) and IRA accounts offer a distinct tax advantage that will allow them to enjoy more of their savings in their later years.

Unfortunately, what those Americans frequently misunderstand is that 401(k)s and IRAs don't eliminate taxes, they postpone taxes – to a future date. That's an important consideration, especially if you believe taxes are going up.

Equally important, the tax calculation on the money growing inside a 401(k) and IRA can also increase, meaning your postponed tax bill could be higher when the money comes out.

Let's examine these two very important tax concepts in a little greater detail.

401(k)s and IRAs are tax-deferred accounts, not tax-free accounts. When you begin to withdraw money from them in retirement, you'll find yourself paying taxes on that money just as though it were a regular paycheck.

To bring that concept down to dollars and cents, let's say "Bob Smith" has accumulated a million dollars in a 401(k) account. That doesn't mean he has a million dollars to spend in retirement. If he's in the 33% tax bracket, Bob will have to "make do" on $670,000, because $330,000 of that money will be going to Uncle Sam.

And that's not the worst of it. When people are asked where they think tax rates will be in their retirement years, many believe they will be higher than they are today. With record federal and state deficits, as well as tax increase talk running through the halls of Congress and the White House, there is little surprise most feel this way.

Yet very few people think about tax rates increasing inside their 401(k)s or IRAs! That can be a very expensive oversight.

The great stock market crash of 2008 caused many of us to rethink our basic approach to our finances. That's a good thing - but it's a rethink that we also need to extend beyond the here and now. The traditional retirement accounts we've been aggressively sold over the past few decades have many shocking drawbacks that will leave many future retirees wondering what hit them...

...or, more precisely, how are they going to maintain a similar standard of living in their retirement years.

The good news is there are alternative methods to saving for retirement that are not only tax-deferred, but also tax-free when you withdraw the money. In this chapter, we'll talk about how to "break the tax code" once and for all when it comes to securing your long-term financial future.

But first, more about deferred taxes and the potential ticking tax bomb growing inside your 401(k) and your IRA.

## Not Enough Money And Too Much Tax

"The ugly truth… is that the 401(k) is a lousy idea, a financial flop, a rotten repository for our retirement reserves." Another harsh statement, right? Well, this time, the above quote doesn't come from us – or even from some 'wacko' internet blog. No, that comes straight from the editors of *TIME* Magazine in their 2009 cover story, "Why it's Time to Retire the 401(k)."

TIME's editors recount how the 401(k) was originally created 30 years ago as an executive perk and another way to dodge the IRS (at least for awhile). It was never meant to take the place of traditional pensions the way that it has. That said, companies quickly saw that the 401(k) was more cost-effective to implement than traditional pensions – so, naturally the business world quickly embraced and offered it to all its workers as they eliminated their defined benefit programs.

Unfortunately, most people simply haven't saved enough money in these kinds of accounts to be able to maintain their current standard of living in retirement. According to a February 19, 2011 article in The *Wall Street Journal (WSJ)*, "the median household headed by a person aged 60 to 62 with a 401(k) account has less than one-quarter of what is needed in that account to maintain its standard of living in retirement." The Journal (WSJ) itself uncovered that startling statistic in a study commissioned at the Center for Retirement Research at Boston College.

We repeat - "Less than one-quarter of what is needed." That's maybe the harshest statement so far, but this one isn't opinion, it's pure fact.

Beyond not having enough money in these accounts, there are

still the eventual taxes to reckon with. Yes, you get a tax deduction at the time you contribute certain funds to a 401(k) – but, as we stated earlier, you will have to pay taxes when you withdraw those funds during retirement.

Additionally, given the backdrop of our government's fiscal obligations, taxes may end up being heftier than if you had simply paid them at the time of your employment. Again, the facts indicate that everyone's tax load is likely going to get heavier, not lighter.

Where are tax rates headed in this country? As of this writing, the tax rates are the lowest they've been since 1958. But America is now drowning in debt – a fact that can no longer be ignored or swept under the rug.

Here's how far underwater we are as a nation at this moment: The National Debt is at 14.5 trillion and counting.

Meanwhile, how much revenue do we have coming in? A little over two trillion.

You don't have to be a CPA to figure out how that shakes out. The U.S. government can only cut so much before they have to start setting the stage for bringing in more revenue. And more revenue usually means levying more taxes on the population, i.e. you and me. Because here's the final depressing figure for you to consider - when you break that 14 1/2 trillion dollar debt down, it comes out to a $129,000 liability for each single U.S. taxpayer.

The bottom line is that many Americans could have far less at retirement than they expect, thanks to the bite of taxes alone.

## The Wall Street Gamble

If all that isn't enough for you, there's more bad news for the 401(k) holder. Let's walk past the two hidden 401(k) realities we've already pulled out into the light – the hefty tax bill and the lack of adequate savings for retirement - and let's move on to one of the biggest single factors influencing these accounts: the stock market.

Where do most men and women have their IRA and 401(k) savings invested? In stocks and mutual funds. As the catastrophic financial events of late 2008 made clear, betting on Wall Street can have dire consequences. During the year and a half after that epic crash, 401(k) and IRA account balances plunged by an average of 31%.

You might say that was a once-in-a-lifetime event. Okay, we'll give you that for the time being. So let's just move on and take the future as a blank slate, examining the three basic options that can happen in the stock market and how it should influence your thinking on the 401(k).

## Option 1: The Stock Market Gains

The economy may gain strength and stocks may start skyrocketing. It's possible. What happens after that spike, however, is what you might want to be concerned about. Consider the market's performance from 2000 to 2010.

The year 2000 began with the S&P 500 hitting 1552.87 in March of that year, its historical high point. Two years later, it had lost almost 50% of its value when the dot-com boom burst, reaching a low of 768.63 in October of 2002. In October of 2007, however, the S&P reached a new peak of 1565.14.

At that point, a whole new bubble was beginning to give way – the subprime mortgage market, which was suddenly toxic. That brought the S&P back down to 752.44 in November of 2008, its lowest close since 1997. A new bottom was reached in March of 2008, with the S&P collapsing to 676.53. As of this writing, the index is hovering around the 1200 mark after a week of extreme volatility, in which it lost roughly 5% of its value. The S&P remains down over 300 points (or over 20%) from its 2000 high.

Bottom line, if future stock gains are like the past 10 years, think of Newton's law of gravity…What goes up could come back down.

## Option #2: The Stock Market Loses

As you can see from our discussion of Option #1, the stock market is definitely a risky bet. You might say, "Well, over time, the market always recovers from its losses." That might be true, but the problem is going to be, especially if you're planning for retirement, whether you have enough time left for that recovery to happen. When you need to start withdrawing the money, you're not going to have the luxury of waiting until the market recovers from a recent plunge.

Again, in the past decade, stocks have ended up below the point where they started. If we hit another "lost decade," will your 401(k) be able to recover in time for your retirement? And will you actually make any gains, or just get your account balance back to where it was when it started?

There are no guarantees, as 401(k) holders discovered in 2002, and again in 2008, when huge bubbles burst and investors were caught off-guard. Some lost over 50% of their holdings – is that a risk worth taking with the money you're saving for those years when you're no longer receiving an income from a job?

## Option #3: The Stock Market Stays Where It Is

Of course, we don't mean the stock market doesn't literally stay where it is. Instead, it goes up a bit…it goes down a bit…without any really significant movement either way. That means, when all is said and done and the numbers are averaged, the market stands still (excluding any dividends you might have received).

And, of course, even if you did "stand still" with the market, that simply means you're not growing your money at all. And isn't growth the whole point of the 401(k)?

The question you might now be asking yourself is, why didn't anyone see these huge problems with 401(k) accounts sooner than this?

Well, as the TIME magazine cover story we referenced earlier points out, 401(k)s are only really being tested for the first time now. Because these types of accounts were just begun in the 1980's, the first wave of retirees relying on them are only now starting to realize that their retirement years might be more of a struggle than they anticipated - if they can actually afford to retire at all. Many will have to continue to work at least part-time.

## Finding A Better Way

What it all comes down to is that the largest generation ever about to retire is facing a rude awakening by not understanding how 401(k)s and IRAs truly work.

So… what's the answer?

Here's what you might want to keep in mind for your own personal planning purposes. These are the principals that make up the major tenets of our tax-free retirement strategies:

*Principle #1: Safety First. Losses are difficult to recover from, so don't put your retirement principal at risk.*

*Principle #2: Ensure You Have Enough. Liquidity and accessibility are imperative.*

*Principle #3: Mitigate and Eliminate Taxes. Everyone focuses on return rates, but the fact is, the biggest drain on your retirement fund is likely to be taxes. Any retirement strategy should have a clear plan for reducing and eliminating them.*

Of course, you might say, if all those goals could be achieved, wouldn't most financial planners already be making those objectives part of their retirement strategies for their clients?

Well, while a few are aware how to make this happen, most have financial incentives to push the more traditional products, either because of who they work for or what commissions they earn.

Even people in HR departments discuss the benefits of in-house 401(k) accounts. But here's an interesting fact you're unlikely to hear from the HR department; there are other retirement savings opportunities that make it possible to not only safeguard your retirement funds, but also get market-like growth without market risk, access your funds anytime - and withdraw tax-free income in retirement. Multi-millionaires and Fortune 500 executives, who can afford expensive tax attorneys and financial advisors, have been using them for years.

But you don't have to be a multi-millionaire to take advantage of those secrets. As a matter of fact, almost anyone can take advantage of these retirement planning alternatives -- that is, as long as you fall into one of the following four categories:

- *You are allocating part of your monthly gross income towards retirement and don't want to outlive your money (or unnecessarily hand it over to the government).*

- *You have received or receive lump-sum payments in the form of a bonus, commission, severance or inheritance that you want to put towards retirement.*

- *You already have enough money for retirement purposes and now want to provide a financial legacy either for heirs or a charity. 401(k)s, IRAs, Roth IRAs and SEPS are not really structured for that goal.*

- *You have one or more old 401(k) and/or IRA accounts that are languishing and not getting much of your time and attention.*

## What A Retirement Fund Should Do For You

The retirement strategies we discuss are neither risky nor new. As noted, they're strategies that have been available to the general public for years, but aren't widely known.

Listed below are some of the enduring benefits they provide. Are you getting these benefits in your retirement account?

### Market Loss Protection

The most unique nature of this strategy is that you will never lose any principal. Yes, you read that right. Your cash value never takes a loss regardless of what the stock market does. Now to be fair, as a tradeoff, you do have to give up some of the upside gains, and like corporate bonds, there is always a small credit risk. But who wouldn't be willing to give up a little bit on the upside for the assurance that your principal will never decrease?

## Gains Are Locked In

Your account balance is reset every year so that, if you make significant gains during the year, those gains are protected; you can't lose them as 401(k) owners did when the stock market crashed. Initial cash contributions are protected as well.

## Tax-Free Access to Accumulating Cash

As mentioned before, we want to make sure you don't lose significant chunks of your retirement savings to Uncle Sam. With our strategies, you not only grow your money tax-deferred, but you are also able to withdraw that money without being taxed. Why give up 25%? ...30%? ...even 40%? ...if you don't have to.

## Avoids Taxes on Social Security Payments

Here's another little IRS fact you may not know about if you haven't started receiving Social Security payments yet. Depending on how much money you're taking out of a 401(k) or IRA (i.e. what your taxable income is after you retire), you may find that a high percentage of your Social Security income is subject to income taxes. The way our retirement strategy works, this is never an issue. You are never penalized by the IRS for accessing your own money.

## No Forced Distribution

With most IRAs and 401(k)s, you have to start withdrawing money shortly after you turn 70. In this case, you can keep your fund growing as long as you want to. You don't have to start liquidating ever – and you can even leave what's in the fund to your children.

## No Age Restrictions

Just as you don't have to start taking out money by a certain age, you also don't have to wait until you're 59 1/2 to start withdrawing the money without incurring a penalty. You also can be any age to utilize this plan – for example, you can set it up it in your children's names so they can make withdrawals.

The above are the "big picture" benefits. Other advantages include the avoidance of probate problems after your death as well as protection from lawsuits in many states, depending on specific state laws.

There's no question that a potential retirement crisis is looming on the horizon – there will be an unprecedented number of retirees in America and many of them will not have the finances to enjoy their retirement dreams.

The good news is there are other retirement options available that provide some of the best features of 401k's and IRA's—without their limitations, penalties and hefty taxes.

Want to learn more? We have a book to help you better understand these retirement planning strategies – and we'll be happy to send you the book for free. Request your complimentary copy at: www.sagefinancialpartners.com.

Someone once said, if everything you knew was in a box…and you heard something new that wasn't in that box…you would have one of two choices to make. You can either choose to ignore it…or you can get a bigger box.

If you are interested in expanding your "box of knowledge" in order to take greater control of your financial future, we invite you to take advantage of the resources at www.sagefinancialpartners.com.

Safe, secure and tax-free retirement savings are possible. We know. It's what we do.

## About Mark

Mark MacDonald is Senior Partner and co-founder of Sage Financial Partners. Mr. MacDonald has been featured on NBC, CBS, ABC and Fox affiliates discussing tax-free retirement planning for individuals and private business owners. In addition to being a best-selling author, Mark is former publisher of Individual Investor magazine.

Mark leads the tax-free retirement practice at Sage Financial Partners. This practice is devoted to the unique retirement and tax planning needs of business owners and individuals who do not want to run out of money in retirement.

To learn how you can secure your financial future via the tax-free products and strategies outlined in this chapter...plus get a complimentary " Retirement Ready or Not" analysis,
email: Request@SageFinancialPartners.com.

Sage Financial Partners is a Registered Investment Advisor and member of FINRA and the Better Business Bureau.

CHAPTER 8

# Home Office Deduction For Your Business – Yes! You Can!

By Peni Ingram, CPA

Several years ago, many business owners were afraid to take a tax deduction for the business use of their home... and for good reason. The IRS was much more likely back then to call for an audit of the business owner's tax return, and deny that deduction. As a matter of fact, there was an example of that very thing happening to a self-employed anesthesiologist. The IRS argued that the anesthesiologist did not see any patients in his home office, and conducted most of his business affairs at the hospital, therefore his office in the home was not a principal place of business and the deduction was denied.

The Tax Court overturned the IRS's denial and granted the home office deduction. The Tax Court determined that the anesthesiologist performed administrative and management activities in his home office, and he did not have any other such office where he conducted these affairs, so they allowed the deduction. After the Tax Court reversed the IRS's decision, the rules for a Home Office business deduction have relaxed and now more and more businesses are able to take this deduction. Several rules apply, however, and you must qualify.

## Principal Place of Business

You can have more than one business location, including your home, for a single trade or business. To qualify to deduct the expenses for the business use of your home under the principal place of business test, your home must be your principal place of business for that trade or business. To determine whether your home is your principal place of business, you must consider:

- *The relative importance of the activities performed at each place where you conduct business, and*

- *The amount of time spent at each place where you conduct business.*

Your home office will qualify as your principal place of business if you meet the following requirements:

- *You use it exclusively and regularly for administrative or management activities of your trade or business.*

- *You have no other fixed location where you conduct substantial administrative or management activities of your trade or business.*

***Administrative or management activities.*** There are many activities that are administrative or managerial in nature. The following are a few examples:

- *Billing customers, clients, or patients.*

- *Keeping books and records.*

- *Ordering supplies.*

- *Setting up appointments.*

- *Forwarding orders or writing reports.*

***Administrative or management activities performed at other locations.*** The following activities performed by you or others will not disqualify your home office from being your principal place of business.

- *You have others conduct your administrative or manage-*

*ment activities at locations other than your home. (For example, another company does your billing from its place of business.)*

• *You conduct administrative or management activities at places that are not fixed locations of your business, such as in a car or a hotel room.*

• *You occasionally conduct minimal administrative or management activities at a fixed location outside your home.*

• *You conduct substantial non-administrative or non-management business activities at a fixed location outside your home. (For example, you meet with or provide services to customers, clients, or patients at a fixed location of the business outside your home.)*

• *You have suitable space to conduct administrative or management activities outside your home, but choose to use your home office for those activities instead.*

The same home office can be the principal place of business for two or more separate business activities. Whether your home office is the principal place of business for more than one business activity must be determined separately for each of your trade or business activities. You must use the home office exclusively and regularly for one or more of the following purposes.

• *As the principal place of business for one or more of your trades or businesses.*

• *As a place to meet or deal with patients, clients, or customers in the normal course of one or more of your trades or businesses.*

• *If your home office is a separate structure, in connection with one or more of your trades or businesses.*

You can use your home office for more than one business activity, **but you cannot use it for any non-business (i.e., personal) activities.**

*Example.* Joe is a self-employed plumber. Most of Joe's time is spent at customers' homes and offices installing and repairing plumbing. He has a small office in his home that he uses exclusively and regularly for the administrative or management activities of his business, such as phoning customers, ordering supplies, and keeping his books.

Joe writes up estimates and records of work completed at his customers' premises. He does not conduct any substantial administrative or management activities at any fixed location other than his home office. Joe does not do his own billing. He uses a local bookkeeping service to bill his customers.

Joe's home office qualifies as his principal place of business for deducting expenses for its use. He uses the home office for the administrative or managerial activities of his plumbing business and he has no other fixed location where he conducts these administrative or managerial activities. His choice to have his billing done by another company does not disqualify his home office from being his principal place of business. He meets all the qualifications, including principal place of business, so he can deduct expenses (to the extent of the deduction limit, explained later) for the business use of his home.

The first thing you must do, in determining your Home Office deduction is to calculate the portion of your home that is used exclusively and regularly for business purposes.

## Business Percentage

To find the business percentage, compare the size of the part of your home that you use for business to your whole house. Use the resulting percentage to figure the business part of the expenses for operating your entire home. You can include in the business part, space used for your office, and space used for storage of inventory, supplies and other business things.

You can use any reasonable method to determine the business percentage. The following are two commonly used methods for figuring the percentage.

*1. Divide the area (length multiplied by the width) used for business by the total area of your home.*

*2. If the rooms in your home are all about the same size, you can divide the number of rooms used for business by the total number of rooms in your home.*

***Example:***

- *Your office is 240 square feet (12 feet × 20 feet).*
- *Your home is 1,200 square feet.*
- *Your office is 20% (240 ÷ 1,200) of the total area of your home.*

## Part-Year Use

You cannot deduct expenses for the business use of your home incurred during any part of the year you did not use your home for business purposes. For example, if you begin using part of your home for business on July 1, and you meet all the tests from that date until the end of the year, consider only your expenses for the last half of the year in figuring your allowable deduction.

## Deduction Limit

Some of your home office expenses can be deducted from net business income, even if it creates a net business loss, such as:

*1. The business part of expenses you could deduct even if you did not use your home for business (such as mortgage interest, real estate taxes, and casualty and theft losses that are allowable as itemized deductions on Schedule A) can be deducted from the net business income (Gross income less business expenses).*

*2. The business expenses that relate to the business activity in the home (for example, business phone, supplies, and depreciation on equipment), but not to the use of the home itself.*

Your deduction of otherwise non-deductible expenses, such as home insurance, utilities, maintenance, cleaning, and depreciation (with depreciation taken last), that are allocable to the business, cannot be greater than the net business income. In other words, you cannot increase your business loss by these deductions.

***Carryover of disallowed expenses.*** If your deductions are greater than the current year's limit, you can carry over the excess to the next year. They are subject to the deduction limit for that year, whether or not you live in the same home during that year.

***NOTE:*** By the way, the reason for the benefit of deducting the business portion of mortgage interest, real estate taxes and casualty and theft losses as a home office deduction, is that it reduces Adjusted Gross Income. If you just deduct those things as an itemized deduction on Schedule A, it would be below the Adjusted Gross Income line, and could cause you to lose other deductions elsewhere on your return. Also, if you have net business income, it reduces Self Employment taxes on your business income.

**TIP** If your home office qualifies as your principal place of business, you can deduct your daily transportation costs between your home and another work location in the same trade or business. A good tip is, to perform some element of work from your home office before you drive to another business location, such as reading business e-mails. For more information on transportation costs, see IRS Publication 463, Travel, Entertainment, Gift, and Car Expenses.

Other expenses are deductible only if you use your home for business. You can use the business percentage of these expenses to figure your total business use of the home deduction. These expenses generally include (but are not limited to) the following:

- *Depreciation (covered under Depreciating Your Home, later).*
- *Insurance.*
- *Rent paid for the use of property you do not own but use*

*in your trade or business.*

• *Repairs.*

• *Security system.*

• *Utilities and services.*

## Casualty Losses

If you have a casualty loss on your home that you use for business, treat the casualty loss as a direct expense, an indirect expense, or an unrelated expense, depending on the property affected:

• *A direct expense is the loss on the portion of the property you use only in your business. Use the entire loss to figure the business use of the home deduction.*

• *An indirect expense is the loss on property you use for both business and personal purposes. Use only the business portion to figure the deduction.*

• *An unrelated expense is the loss on property you do not use in your business. Do not use any of the loss to figure the deduction.*

If you are filing Schedule C (Form 1040), get Form 8829 and follow the instructions for casualty losses.

Also complete Form 4684, Casualties and Thefts, to report your loss. You complete both section A (Personal Use Property) and section B (Business and Income-Producing Property) as your home is used both for business and personal purposes.

## Repairs

The cost of repairs that relate to your business is a deductible expense. For example, a furnace repair benefits the entire home. If you use 10% of your home for business, you can deduct 10% of the cost of the furnace repair.

Repairs keep your home in good working order over its useful life. Examples of common repairs are patching walls and floors, painting, wallpapering, repairing roofs and gutters, and mending leaks. However, repairs are sometimes treated as a permanent improvement and are not deductible. See Permanent improvements, later, under Depreciating Your Home.

## Security System

If you install a security system that protects all the doors and windows in your home, you can deduct the business percentage of the expenses you incur to maintain and monitor the system. You also can take a depreciation deduction for the part of the cost of the security system relating to the business use of your home.

## Utilities and Services

Expenses for utilities and services, such as electricity, gas, trash removal, and cleaning services, are generally personal expenses. If you use part of your home for business, you can deduct the business part of these expenses. It is the same as the percentage of your home used for business.

*Telephone* - The basic local telephone service charge, including taxes, for the first telephone line into your home (i.e., landline) is a non-deductible personal expense, unless you use that line for a business FAX. However, charges for business long-distance phone calls on that line, as well as the cost of a second line into your home used exclusively for business, are deductible business expenses. Do not include these expenses as a cost of using your home for business. Deduct these charges separately on the appropriate form or schedule. For example, if you file Schedule C (Form 1040), deduct these expenses on line 25, Utilities (instead of line 30, Expenses for business use of your home).

## Depreciating your Home

Before you figure your depreciation deduction, you need to know the following information:

- *The month and year you started using your home for business.*

- *The adjusted basis and fair market value of your home (excluding land) at the time you began using it for business.*

- *The cost of any improvements before and after you began using the property for business.*

- *The percentage of your home used for business. See Business Percentage, earlier.*

**Adjusted basis defined.** The adjusted basis of your home is generally its cost, plus the cost of any permanent improvements you made to it, minus any casualty losses or depreciation deducted in earlier tax years. For a discussion of adjusted basis, see IRS Publication 551.

**Permanent improvements.** A permanent improvement increases the value of property, adds to its life, or gives it a new or different use. Examples of improvements are replacing electric wiring or plumbing, adding a new roof or addition, paneling, or remodeling. The cost of permanent improvements is depreciated over 39 years, just like the cost of the home is.

You must carefully distinguish between repairs and improvements. See **Repairs**, earlier. You also must keep accurate records of these expenses. These records will help you decide whether an expense is a deductible expense or a capital (added to the basis) improvement. However, if you make repairs as part of an extensive remodeling or restoration of your home, the entire job is an improvement.

If you began using your home for business for the first time in 2010, depreciate the business part as non-residential real property under the modified accelerated cost recovery system (MACRS). Under MACRS, non-residential real property is depreciated using the straight-line method over 39 years. For more information on MACRS and other methods of depreciation, see IRS Publication 946.

So, don't fear taking this valid deduction on your tax return as a **Business Use of your Home deduction.** I tell my clients to look at it this way: If you were to have your primary business office outside of your home, all of the costs of running and maintaining that office would be a deductible business expense, so your home office is no different!

## About Peni

Peniruth (Peni) Ingram is a Certified Public Accountant who has 26 years of experience working in public accounting firms as a senior auditor and tax expert. She is now using this experience in her own practice doing audit, accounting and tax preparation. She recognizes that in this busy world, there are many business owners who have an expertise in providing goods and services to their customers, but haven't the time or ability to maintain their financial recordkeeping and are looking for solutions. She offers the right solutions to businesses in need.... And with a smile!

Peniruth (Peni) Ingram earned her degree in Accounting at California State University, Fullerton, CA. She is a member of the Tennessee Society of Certified Public Accountants and Board Treasurer of the Greater Cool Springs Chamber of Commerce, providing complimentary bookkeeping and tax services for the Chamber.

When she is not crunching numbers, her hobbies include playing Appalachian Dulcimer folk music and old time string band music with her husband and friends.

If you need an accountant who cares about your financial well-being, call Peni Ingram at 615-364-8035.

# CHAPTER 9

# How To Deduct Your Kid's Braces

By Jeramy Smith, CPA

## HEALTH REIMBURSEMENTS ARRANGEMENT – CODE SECTION 105

**M**y clients are always asking "What all can I deduct? Can I deduct my car, phones, clothes, dry cleaning, my kid's braces, etc?" Surprising to some, the answer is more often "it depends" rather than an outright "no." How the "it depends" changes into a "yes" is largely a product of pro-active tax planning. In other words, planning and setting up your business, benefits, etc, in such a way that you can take advantage of different areas of the tax code. This chapter addresses one area of the tax code (Code Section 105) that allows a business to deduct otherwise non-deductible health-care related expenses.

I had a client (names and medical expenses have been changed to protect the innocent!) tell me that his teenager needed braces. He asked me if there was any way he could deduct those upcoming expenses. At first glance, that may seem like a completely personal expense that would be very hard to justify as a business deduction, but with proper planning, I will be able to answer the question with a resounding "YES!" Imagine his surprise when I said "Actually, yes, there is a way that your business can deduct that – from both income tax and self-employment tax!" Because of the way his business was set up and because his wife worked as the office manager taking care of daily tasks, appointment setting, travel arrangements, etc., he fit a set of circumstances that allowed him to set up a Section 105 Health Reimbursement Arrangement. (This would also work for out-of-pocket expenses paid for prescriptions, co-pays, deductibles, hospital stays, dental, vision, hearing, plus many others.)

A Health Reimbursement Arrangement (HRA) allows a qualified business to reimburse its employees, their spouses, and their dependents for uninsured, out-of-pocket medical costs. These reimbursements are deductible by the company, but are NOT taxable to the employee.

Let me give you a brief overview of how this works. In general, your business has a W-2 employee and you wish to offer that employee this benefit. You set up the plan including the maximum amount that you want to reimburse per year. The combination of the cash W-2 wages plus benefits must be reasonable compensation for the work that they do.

## HOW DO I SET UP AND ADMINISTER THIS?

I personally refer my clients to a Third Party Administrator (TPA) that does most of the work to set up and maintain these plans at a very reasonable cost. I do that for three reasons:

1. In all honesty, it's probably cheaper than I could provide the same service myself, but since this is all the TPA does, and since they do it all day every day, they are able to do it more efficiently while making sure every "t" is crossed and every "i" is dotted.

2. I also prefer using the TPA since they continually stay up on the laws and make sure their plans are solid and audit-proof.

3. They have an audit guarantee and a savings guarantee.

For example, *The Patient Protection and Affordable Care Act* includes a catalog of comprehensive healthcare reforms that will fundamentally change the way everyone does business. In order to receive the maximum tax savings available through these plans, you will now need to adhere to a stricter set of rules and regulations. These new regulations are complex, exacting, and difficult to understand. The company I use not only makes sure the plan is compliant, but they also keep me up-to-date, so that I can help guide my clients and help them protect their tax savings.

## WHAT ALL DO I NEED TO DO?

I would highly suggest you use a Third Party Administrator who specializes in these plans.

Note: I had another client who wanted to set up a Health Reimbursement Arrangement, but didn't want to pay the few hundred dollars it was going to cost him, even though it was going to result in an over $4,000 tax savings in his first year. Instead, he spent hours online reading and finding documentation to try to set up the plan on his own. Had he used the Third Party Administrator I work with, I would know, absolutely, that his plan was solid and audit proof. In fact, the TPA I use has an **"audit guarantee"** because they know, absolutely, that their plans are within the laws of the IRS.

At the time I am writing this, they have a **"savings guarantee."** If you do not deduct at least $2,000 in a plan year, you will receive a full refund of your enrollment fee. So there is really no risk to see how much you can save.

In general, these are the items you will need to do and the TPA can help you with these:

- Have a written plan and send out Summary Plan Benefits
- Have a legitimate employee and employment contract
- Establish the compensation package
- Pay a W-2 Wage monthly or quarterly

- Reimburse Medical Expenses
- Submit benefit expenses annually to your Third Party Administrator

## WHO IS THE BEST CANDIDATE FOR THIS:

In my opinion, the absolute best candidate for these plans are small family-owned businesses who can legitimately hire a spouse to take advantage of the available benefits, and have enough medical expenses to make the numbers work in their favor.

But even if your business has other non-family employees, this could still be an excellent tool, as it could help you offer benefits to your employees that are non-taxable to them, and still result in a deduction for you.

Go to my website, follow the links to the company I use, and see if you qualify and find out how much you might be able to save in taxes.

## DOES THIS WORK IF I AM SELF-EMPLOYED?

It can, depending on your entity type and if your spouse is an employee of yours. Let me briefly cover how this works in different types of entities, although **ALL entities** can recognize some tax savings based on their facts – so get an estimated calculation done for your company, no matter what kind of entity it is.

### SOLE PROPRIETOR:
The taxpayer owns the company. He can hire his spouse to do the bookkeeping for his company and provide a compensation package that includes a W-2 wage, reimbursement of family medical insurance, and reimbursement of family out-of-pocket costs.

### PARTNERSHIPS:
Let's say Mark and Craig own a business as a partnership. They can both hire their spouses and get the same treatment as the sole proprietor above.

## C-CORPORATIONS:

A single person operating out of a C-Corporation can get the same benefits as the sole proprietor above. Spousal employment is NOT required in a C-Corporation.

## S-CORPORATIONS:

The benefit is not as large since both the S-Corporation owner and his spouse are treated as self employed, but there is still a benefit. All benefits that go through the plan can escape the Self-employment tax. This works in a similar way to how health insurance is reported and treated for S-Corporation owners, however, only the health insurance is deducted in calculating the income tax as well. Depending on your expenses, this could still result in significant savings.

## LLC:

You have to look at how the LLC files its taxes. It uses the method above based on how it files its taxes.

# AM I NOT ALREADY DEDUCTING MY MEDICAL EXPENSES?

The answer is yes...and no. It just depends on all of your facts and circumstances, but the general answer is that very few people actually get much tax benefit from their medical expenses.

# INSURANCE PREMIUMS

If you are self-employed, or treated as self-employed based on how your business entity is set up, you are probably deducting your health insurance premium on page 1 of your 1040, so you are saving tax at your marginal tax rate. So, $10,000 in insurance premiums would lower your taxes $2,500 if you were in the 25% marginal tax bracket.

(NOTE: For 2010 only, The Small Business Tax Act of 2010 allowed self-employed taxpayers to deduct self-employed health insurance for both Income Tax AND for self-employment tax. This currently only applies to 2010, but that is something to watch out for.)

By getting the premiums into a Health Reimbursement Arrangement, many entity types can also save Social Security and Medicare tax (another 15.3%) in addition to the marginal Income Tax rate mentioned above.

## OTHER OUT-OF-POCKET COSTS

Any other allowable health care expenses are typically deducted on Schedule A – Itemized Deductions, but many people never realize any true tax savings from their Schedule A. For health care expenses to make a difference on Schedule A, there are 2 hurdles to overcome.

1. You can only include the out-of-pocket costs OVER 7.5% of your adjusted gross income (that will eventually change to 10% under the new health care bill).

2. That excess is then added to your other itemized deductions like Mortgage Interest, Real Estate Taxes, and Contributions. That total sum must then be more than your corresponding "Standard Deduction" for you to benefit by taking the Itemized deductions.

So, in reality, many out-of-pocket costs aren't deducted at all, and if they are, they are only for the Income Tax calculation and not for Social Security and Medicare tax.

## SO, GET TO THE POINT...
## HOW MUCH CAN I SAVE???

Let's look at an example and see the potential tax savings:

Joe had a plumbing business that he operates as a sole proprietor (files Schedule C). His wife Judy works in his office part-time scheduling appointments, sending invoices, collecting payments, making deposits at bank, etc.

Joe's health insurance premiums for himself, his wife, and his 2 kids is $600/month, or $7,200 per year.

In addition, the family pays about $5,000 for out-of-pocket medical costs each year (co-pays, deductible amounts, braces, prescriptions, etc.).

Without a section 105 plan, the $12,200 Joe pays for insurance and out-of-pocket expenses would only save Joe about $1,080 in taxes.

If Joe were to restructure these expenses and implement a Section 105, Health Reimbursement Arrangement, the $12,200 Joe pays out could instead result in tax savings of around $4,270. **That's over $3,000 in real tax savings by running the same expenses through a proper Section 105 – Health Reimbursement Arrangement.**

| Before having a 105 HRA plan | | With a 105 HRA plan | |
|---|---|---|---|
| Insurance Premiums | 7,200 | Insurance Premiums | 7,200 |
| Federal Tax Rate | | Federal, State, SE taxes rate | |
| assume 15% marginal tax | x15% | assume 35% tax rate (b) | x35% |
| Tax Savings | 1.080 | Tax Savings | 2.520 |
| Out of Pocket Costs (a) | 5,000 | Out of Pocket Costs (a) | 5,000 |
| No deduction for these | - | Federal, State, SE taxes rate-35% | x35% |
| Tax Savings | - | Tax Savings | 1.750 |
| Total Expenses | 12,200 | Total Expenses | 12,200 |
| Total Deductions | 7,200 | Total Deductions | 12,200 |
| Total Tax Savings | 1.080 | Total Tax Savings | 4.270 |

(a) prescriptions, co-pays, braces, etc

(b) Self employment tax = 15.3%, estimate state tax = 4.7%, federal tax rate = 15%

## SO WHAT SHOULD YOU DO NOW?

I would highly recommend that you go to my website for more information. From there, you can get in contact with the Third Party Administrator that I use and let them work with you to get an estimate of how much you might be able to save. From there, it is just a cost/benefit analysis. Figure out what all your costs would be to set up and administer the plan, and compare that with how much you could save. My guess is that many businesses would benefit from this plan, and the result would be extra cash in your pockets!

Visit now: www.105info.com

## ABOUT JERAMY

If you're like most small business owners, you waste thousands of dollars every year in taxes you don't need to pay. Jeramy Smith wants to help you fix that.

Jeramy Smith has been a CPA in Texas since 1994. He has worked in small public accounting firms as well as in the tax department of a multi-billion dollar Dallas-based holding corporation that owned and operated businesses across a diverse range of industries.

He holds both a Bachelor's and Master's degree from Texas A&M University. He is a member of the American Institute of Certified Public Accountants, the Texas Society of Certified Public Accountants, and the National Association of Tax Professionals. He is also a QuickBooks ProAdvisor.

Education runs deep in his family. In recent years he has focused his tax work on teaching small business clients about tax-saving opportunities and helping them implement real tax-saving strategies.

In the summer of 2010, he started his own accounting firm, Jeramy Smith, CPA, PLLC in the north Dallas suburb of Plano. He agrees that many accountants do a fine job recording the history given to them. They compile monthly, quarterly, and annual books and records. At tax time, they put the "right" numbers in the "right" boxes in the "right" forms. But then they call it a day.

Jeramy doesn't want to just record your history; he wants to help you write it in a proactive manner. In order to minimize your taxes, you need to plan. You need concepts and strategies that leave more on your bottom line.

Mistakes and missed opportunities can cost your small business thousands in additional taxes. Jeramy will help you find those mistakes and missed opportunities and he'll provide solutions to rescue those wasted dollars.

For more information or to contact him visit his webpage: www.planotaxteam.com or email him at: jeramy@planotaxteam.com.

Remember to also visit his Section 105-Health Reimbursement Website at: www.105info.com.

# CHAPTER 10

# How to Stay Out of Trouble With the IRS

*(and What To Do If You Already Are....)*

## By Darrin Mish, Esq.

I f you are a small business owner, then chances are you have owed the IRS taxes at some point in time. If you haven't then it's only a matter of time, unless of course you follow the suggestions in this chapter. It's really unfair because they don't teach us how to take care of our tax obligations in college, or even law school! The government just assumes that small business owners know what they're doing, or maybe something more sinister is afoot. Did you know that the IRS has over 150 penalties at it's disposal when you make a mistake in preparing, filing or paying your taxes? And that's before we even start talking about interest on top of unpaid taxes. Suffice it to say, tax liabilities owed to the IRS grow fast, and don't stop until they're paid (or you manage to avoid paying in full by filing an Offer in Compromise or filing bankruptcy).

Winston Churchill once said *"Let our advance worrying become advance thinking and planning."* This statement is never truer than with taxes. Since the preparation of taxes is one of American's most dreaded annual rituals, it is fair to say that we should attempt to make the best of the situation and be smart about our planning.

The best way to preplan for taxes, especially for an individual, is to make estimated tax payments. This will alleviate the burden of a large tax bill and reduce it to a quarterly payment that you can more easily manage. Since I have been practicing tax law for almost the last two decades, I have seen many clients who could have prevented their entire tax burden by making estimated tax payments. Instead, they allowed the situation to spiral out of control, and beyond their reach to resolve the matter on their own. With added penalties and interest accruing from unpaid tax debts, they have turned small liabilities over a number of years into six-figure tax burdens. The first piece of advice that I give them is START making estimated tax payments and then we will fix the outstanding balances.

Lets assume for a minute that we were talking about first aid. In the case of bleeding, one must first attend to the bleeding and stop it before remedying the wound. Failure to do so will ultimately result in the death of the person. If you already have unpaid taxes, then you are going to have to treat the making of estimated tax payments as the triage you need. If you try to negotiate a settlement, payment plan or other collection alternatives, the IRS will look at your problem and your increasing liabilities much like bleeding. If you leave this important factor in your situation unresolved, the IRS will know how to stop the bleeding …with pressure! The reality is the past can be overcome, but you MUST STOP allowing new IRS liabilities to accrue.

In order to plug the money hole, the IRS can require an individual to make estimated tax payments. If an individual fails to do so, the IRS will impose penalties for the failure to make timely payments. Generally, taxpayers who anticipate they will owe taxes in the upcoming year should ensure that their withholdings and/or estimated tax payments will equal more than 90% of the anticipated liability. If you are unable to do so, you will discover that many of the collection alternatives discussed later in this chapter are not available to you at the negotiation table. Staying current and compliant going forward is imperative; without this commitment the IRS sees you as a continued liability and knows that there is no benefit to negotiating with you – as the problem will only be perpetuated. This is certainly not an admirable position to be in as a taxpayer, though understandably logical from the viewpoint of the IRS.

In determining your requirement with regard to estimated payments, the IRS will factor in your last year's tax return liability and current withholdings from your paycheck. For a small business, they will also use your profit and loss statement. You can determine the same information by completing a current year estimated tax form. Detailed instructions and additional information regarding estimated taxes can be found on Form 1040-ES for the current year. You can download this form and obtain up-to-date information about deadlines, exceptions and payment options at: http://www.irs.gov

Wage earners can submit a new Form W-4 to your employer, therefore adjusting your withholdings and eliminating the need to pay estimated tax payments. The Form W-4 also includes a worksheet to help you determine the correct amount of withholding that you should be deducting from each paycheck. Form W-4 can be found at: http://www.irs.gov

Any corporation that is required to make estimated tax payments will need to download the Form 1120-W to figure the required payment amounts. You can read the IRS Publication 542 for more information regarding the requirements of a corporation. This usually is not applicable if you have the most common sort of small business corporation called a Sub S corporation. Since the Sub S is a 'flow thru' entity – meaning the individual shareholders are taxed on the profits of the corporation – the Sub S typically owes no tax, and therefore has no need to make its own Estimated Tax Payments.

You have the option of paying your Estimated Tax Payments by a variety of methods. An individual can submit the payments with a payment voucher that is attached within the

Form 1040 ES worksheet. You will need to mail your tax payment and form to the Internal Revenue Service address indicated on the 1040-ES form. When mailing payments, you must indicate in the memo line your social security number, tax form and year for the payment to be applied correctly. An individual may also use the EFTPS (electronic federal tax payment system). You must obtain a pin number by applying to the IRS to use this feature, but it can be a convenient way to make timely payments at your leisure.

In 2011, most companies and businesses are required to make all payments by the EFTPS system. Companies and small business who fail to meet this requirement could be subject to additional penalties. If you are wondering if Estimated Tax Payments apply to you, the IRS has a Publication 505 that is available for download from their website. The basic formula for determining if you owe estimated tax payments, before a penalty of under withholding is an issue, is to determine if you owe less than $1000 in tax or if you have paid at least 90% of your current taxes or 100% of your prior tax year's liability.

There will be individuals who cannot use the typical method of paying quarterly tax returns. If your income fluctuates drastically, the determination of estimated tax payments may be more difficult. You can use Form 2210 from the IRS to attach to your Form 1040 at the end of the year. This form will allow you to possibly determine alternative circumstances that could forgive any penalty for failure to pay your estimated tax payments

Over the years representing thousands of taxpayers, a significant number of these clients could have easily avoided the heartache that an IRS problem brings simply by making estimated tax payments. I understand that it's easier said than done. Often times the problem was caused by pure ignorance of the obligation to make quarterly payments; thinking that they "will catch up in the future," or that it would be a better use of the funds to just pay the entire tax debt at the end of the year. All of these reasons are 'off base.' As a small business owner myself, I know how it is. There is always a better use for the money today for the business rather than paying it over to the IRS. But I have come up with a solution that works for me and has worked for many of my clients over the years.

Many years ago, when just starting my law practice, I had an IRS problem of my own. It was under $10,000, but at the time I felt it was impossible to deal with, and I had no idea how I was ever going to get out from under the debt. I was newly married and like many people in this situation, I hid it from my spouse. One day the pressure became too great, and I told my wife what was going on. She was very understanding and came up with a solution that I use to this day and have advised hundreds of clients to utilize as well. You see, most taxpayers see that the estimated payments are due quarterly, and just assume that they cannot be made more frequently. Nothing could be farther from the truth. You can make estimated payments to the IRS every day if you like. The advice goes like this. If you are a sole proprietor or if you're taking distributions from your Sub S Corporation, take 25-30% off the top when you pay yourself. Then you either segregate this money into a separate bank account to be paid to the IRS quarterly, or if you have trouble saving money, send it to the IRS on a Estimated Tax coupon as often as you like. This could be daily, weekly, monthly or whenever you pay yourself. Is this the magic bullet? No. But it keeps you in the ballpark. If you follow this regimen and only have income from the business, you should be much better off than if you didn't make any estimated tax payments at all.

However, if you do find yourself with a tax obligation, one of the most important tips, nuggets or pieces of advice is, when choosing between paying past due taxes or current taxes always pay current tax first. Let me say that again. Always pay current taxes before paying past due taxes. You must show goodwill through becoming compliant if you hope to negotiate past offences. I know that this adjustment to income can be difficult and seems almost impossible. I also know from experience that self-imposed triage is easier than when the IRS demands a remedy! Having a plan in place, even if not immediately realistic, can go a long way at the negotiation table!

There are six alternatives to collection by the IRS if you find yourself with a tax bill larger than you can afford to pay. They are:

1. Installment Agreement
2. Offer in Compromise
3. Waiting for the Collection Statute of Limitations on Collection to expire
4. Bankruptcy
5. Innocent Spouse
6. Hardship Status

#1. An **Installment Agreement** is exactly what it sounds like. It's a payment arrangement with the IRS. If you owe under $10,000 and can pay off the debt within 3 years, the IRS must grant you an installment agreement (unless you have had a prior installment agreement in preceding years). If you owe under $25,000 and full pay the liability within 5 years, they may grant you an installment agreement without requiring that you submit exhaustive financial reports of your personal and business affairs.

#2. An **Offer in Compromise** is when you are able to make a deal with the IRS. In certain situations, when the IRS determines that their best deal would be to take some money from you now rather than try to collect all the money over time, it's possible to make a deal for pennies on the dollar. This is an exhaustive process, requiring significant investigation. It works well for people with no assets and a low income. I have personally settled $99,000 debts for $1,000 but every taxpayer's situation varies. These are not simple cases and may require an attorney to help you through the process.

#3. The **Collection Statute of Limitations** for **Collection** is actually a secret that the IRS keeps from us as taxpayers. In short, the IRS has ten years from the date of the assessment of the tax to collect it. In a typical situation, if you file a tax return with a balance due, the tax is assessed at the time of filing and the IRS then has only ten years to collect. Of course, there are different situations where taxes are assessed much later than when the return is filed. One such situation is in the typical audit scenario. In this scenario, the tax return is filed and selected for audit two years later. The audit takes six months or a year and then the additional tax is assessed. This results in a practical situation where the IRS has over ten years from the date of the filing of the return but still only had ten years from the assessment of the tax.

This is usually not a great tool if the tax years in question are rather recent, but can be great if the tax debt is older. For example, if you have a balance with only 3 years remaining on the collection statute and the IRS decides to put you into an installment agreement, they can decide to give you a payment that will NOT full pay the liability during those three years. This is called a partial pay installment agreement and could result in a taxpayer paying only a fraction of the total.

#4. Most people (including bankruptcy attorneys) don't know that personal income taxes can be discharged in **bankruptcy** if the circumstances are just right. There are five factors to consider when determining whether income tax liabilities are dischargeable in bankruptcy.

1. It must have been more than three years from the due date of the return including extensions.

2. The tax returns, if filed late, must have been filed for more than 2 years.

3. The tax must have been assessed for more than 240 days.

4. The tax return must have been non-fraudulent.

5. Taxpayer must not have been guilty of willful attempt to evade or defeat the tax.

This is highly technical subject matter here. It is advisable that you consult an attorney very familiar with this subject matter. A tiny mistake could result in the filing of a bankruptcy that fails to discharge your tax obligation. This could be catastrophic and is to be avoided at all costs.

#5. **Innocent Spouse** is a remedy used by taxpayers who assert that the tax obligation is or should be the obligation of their former spouse and not their own. It is highly technical, and is a poorly written law in my opinion. If you used to be married, and believe that your former spouse should be held responsible for the tax debt, it's worth looking into.

#6. Lastly, we have **hardship status.** If the IRS determines that you have no ability to pay your tax debt, they may place you in hardship status (also known as *currently not collectible*). During this time, penalties and interest do continue to accrue, but the statute of limitations for collection and the time limitations for bankruptcy also continue to run. This can be used to better situate yourself in order to get the best resolution possible, without the requirement to make monthly payments.

In conclusion, IRS problems can be very tough to resolve. The best course of action is to avoid them by making estimated tax payments. If it's too late to avoid a tax bill, get current by making estimated tax payments if necessary and then consider the six collection alternatives discussed above. Typically, these problems can be resolved without a total disruption of your personal and financial life.

## About Darrin

Darrin Mish, Esq. graduated from Golden Gate University, in San Francisco, California in 1993 with a Doctor of Jurisprudence. He was admitted to the Florida Bar in that same year and the Bar of the State of Colorado in 2002. He has earned an AV rating from Martindale-Hubbell, the country's most popular attorney rating service. An AV rating signifies an attorney that has "achieved the highest levels of professional skill and integrity." The AV rating is based upon peer reviews by other members of the Bar and the judiciary. Lawyers and judges in the larger community have been polled by Martindale-Hubbell and, based upon their submissions, the company has granted him the highest available rating for his legal skills, as well as for honesty and integrity. He has been honored to have his name placed in Martindale-Hubbell's Bar Register of Preeminent Lawyers as well.

This means that you, the client, receive aggressive representation from a young, energetic, honest, yet experienced attorney. Mr. Mish is permitted to practice before the United States Supreme Court; all courts of the State of Florida; the State of Colorado; the United States District Court, Middle District of Florida; United States Court of Appeals, 11th Circuit; United States Tax Court; United States Court of Federal Claims; the United States Court of Appeals, Federal Circuit; United States Court of Appeals, District of Columbia Circuit; and the United States District Court, Northern District of Florida. He has taken the extra steps to be admitted before all of these courts because he is committed to helping you with your IRS problems, including appeals.

In 2002, Mr. Mish was awarded "Practitioner of the Year" by the American Society of IRS Problem Solvers. He is a member of the Tax Freedom Institute, the American Bar Association, the National Association of Tax Professionals, the National Association of Criminal Defense Lawyers, the Florida Association of Criminal Defense Lawyers, and the Hillsborough County Bar Association. These memberships help him stay current with the law and enable him to protect your rights.

# CHAPTER 11

# Owning a Business
## – The Last LEGAL Tax Shelter
## Left in America

By Dominique Molina, CPA, CTC

### The Tax Shelter Concept

"Tax shelters" have been taboo ever since the modern national income tax was established in 1913. Desperate to find relief from paying "their fair share," devious taxpayers began looking for ways to escape the tax code. The names and faces have changed over the years, but the creators of these schemes abuse the boundaries of the tax law, manipulating many unsuspecting victims who are lured into the idea of reducing their greatest expense. It has become such a huge epidemic that the Senate estimates that so-called tax shelters cost the US government over one hundred billion dollars a year in lost tax revenues. The IRS even has a special unit whose sole purpose is to eliminate the countless numbers of tax shelters, attacking the logic used in their creation, and using the court system to render financial punishments to anyone daring to participate in these schemes. For this reason, I hesitate to use the term "tax shelter" to describe the amazing tax benefits available to business owners. Yet there are just no other words, which convey the power of being "sheltered" from the burdens of an expensive tax bill. Therefore,

I'm including in this chapter title the terminology "…last *legal* tax shelter". You will learn, when applied correctly, a business using a solid tax plan will legally help you shelter your income well within the bounds of the law. The best part is, you will be able to sleep at night knowing that you've done everything possible to reduce your risk of an audit, and more importantly, eliminate any negative risk in an audit.

## Concepts to Increasing Your Wealth

There are two basic concepts in aspiring to make more money. First, you can seek to earn more. Yet this presents a challenge as most Americans *are* seeking to earn more, yet most rarely do so (aside from annual cost of living increases). This is an especially challenging pursuit now, in these difficult economic times. The harsh reality may be that you are watching your earnings dwindle. Layoffs are rampant, and Americans find themselves doing more and making less, as employers struggle to stay afloat with pay cuts and work furloughs. Seeking to earn more is an arduous and unpredictable process. What will you do? How will you do it? When will you do it? You can *say* you'd like to earn more money, but the question is, "*can* you earn more money?" On the other hand, you can choose a defensive approach. Financial *defense* is spending less. For most Americans, taxes are our biggest expense. Therefore, it makes sense to focus your financial defense where you spend the most. Sure, you can save 15% on car insurance by switching to GEICO. But how much will that really save in the long run? Financial defense, particularly in the area of tax planning, guarantees results. You can spend all sorts of time, effort, and money promoting your business or working towards promotions at work, but that can't guarantee results. .

So how do you reduce your tax and keep more of what you earn? Or even better, how can you earn more without paying tax? These questions can be answered by looking to the wisest investors and financial experts for advice.

One of the most interesting times of year comes for me when

famed Billionaire, Warren Buffet, announces each tax season the percentage of tax he pays in comparison to his secretary. You may be surprised to discover that it is the humble secretary, earning just $60,000 each year in salary, who pays almost twice the tax rate of one of the world's wealthiest men.

How can this be? Is it positive proof of all the rumors that the wealthy pay very little tax while the burden of providing for our government falls on the middle class? And why does Mr. Buffet disclose this secret each year to the public?

Warren Buffet discloses this information to the public to demonstrate that owning a business and taking advantage of every available tax break is the best way to increase your wealth. Business owners have the most opportunity to create cash and wealth from an idea rather than a task. Even better, they have the most loopholes, deductions, credits, and tax breaks available for them. This combination of benefits creates the possibility of *earning* more and *keeping* more through tax planning.

The reason the wealthy pay less in tax is not because of how *much* money they earn. Rather it is because of *how* they earn it. It is a myth that the rich pay less in tax simply because they are rich. They pay less in tax because they have knowledge; and they can afford the right team of people to provide this knowledge. You can do what the rich do by having a plan and a method for keeping more of what you earn. Owning a business provides the method and unlocks the door to limitless ideas for reducing your tax bill.

## Overview of the Tax System

Let's start by taking a quick look at how the tax system works. This will "lay a foundation" for understanding the specific strategies you'll be learning about in this book.

The process starts with income. This includes most of what you'd think the IRS is interested in:

- Earned income from wages, salaries, bonuses, and commissions.

- Profits and losses from your own business.

- Interest and dividends from bank accounts, stocks, bonds, and mutual funds.

- Capital gains from property sales.

- Pensions, IRAs, and annuity income.

- Alimony and gambling winnings.

- Even illegal income is taxable. The IRS doesn't care how you make it; they just want their share! (The good news is, if you're operating an illegal business, you can deduct the same expenses as if you were running a legitimate business. If you're a bookie, you can deduct the cost of a cell phone you use to take bets.)

Once you've added up total income, it's time to start subtracting. You start with what are called, "adjustments to income." These are a group of special deductions, listed on the first page of Form 1040, that you can take whether you itemize deductions or not. Total income minus adjustments to income equals "adjusted gross income" or "AGI." Adjustments to income are also called "above the line" deductions, because you take them "above" AGI. Adjustments include IRA contributions, moving expenses, half of your self-employment tax, self-employed health insurance, Keogh and SEP contributions, alimony you pay, and student loan interest.

Once you've determined adjusted gross income, you can take a standard deduction or itemized deductions, whichever is greater. The standard deduction is $5,700** for single taxpayers, $8,400** for heads of households, $11,400** for joint filers, and $5,700** each for married couples filing separately. Tax deductions reduce your taxable income. If you're in the 15% bracket, an extra dollar of deductions cuts your tax by 15 cents. If you're in the 35% bracket, that same extra dollar of deductions cuts your tax by 35 cents.

You can also deduct a personal exemption of $3,650** for yourself, your spouse, and any dependents.

Once you've subtracted deductions and personal exemptions, you have arrived at taxable income. At this stage of your tax return, the table of tax brackets tells you how much to pay. Its just a matter of simple math.

You may also owe self-employment tax, which replaces Social Security and Medicare for sole proprietors, partnerships, and LLCs. You'll also owe state and local income and earnings taxes.

Finally, you'll subtract any tax credits. These are dollar-for-dollar tax reductions, regardless of your tax bracket. So if you're in the 15% bracket, a dollar's worth of tax credit cuts your tax by a full dollar. If you're in the 35% bracket, an extra dollar's worth of tax credit cuts your tax by the same dollar. There's no secret to tax credits, other than knowing what's out there. It's worth mentioning at this point that many of current administration's tax proposals involve tax credits, so these will likely become an even more important part of your tax planning.

Ultimately, there are two kinds of dollars in this world: pre-tax dollars, and after-tax dollars.

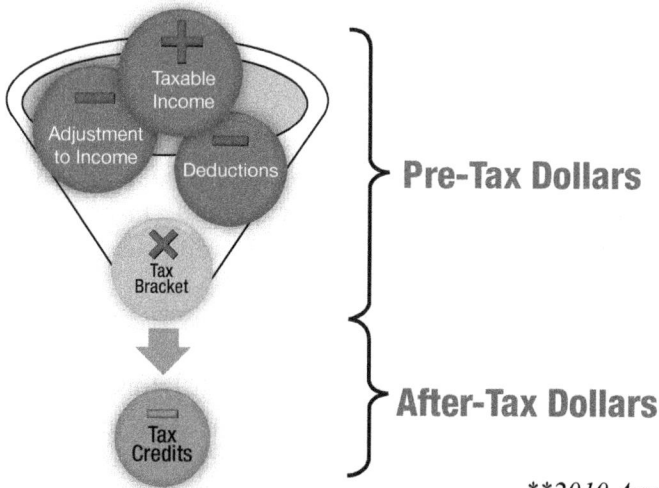

**Pre-Tax Dollars**

**After-Tax Dollars**

*\*\*2010 Amounts*

Pre-tax dollars are great. And after-tax dollars aren't bad. But they're not as good as pre-tax dollars. The bottom line is:

**You lose every time you spend after-tax dollars that could have been pre-tax dollars.**

Subsequently, one of the key components to tax planning is the ability to shift after tax dollars into pre-tax dollars.

The problem with most middle-income taxpayers is they fall onto the endless hamster wheel of taxes and spending. They work hard, do well in school, get a good job at a stable company, pay their taxes first through paycheck withholding, and spend whatever is left over.

## Employee Spending Cycle

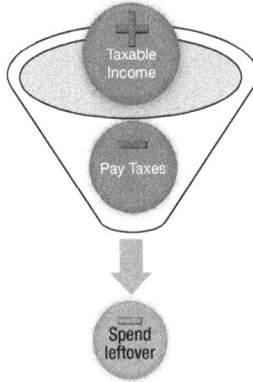

When you are an employee, the government takes its share first; with each and every paycheck. Your ability to provide for your expenses rests in whatever amount is leftover.

On the other hand, the real key to paying a lot less in tax is learning how to shift your after tax dollars into pre-tax dollars. Owning a business provides a legal way to accomplish this. When set up correctly, a business pays its expenses first, and then pays tax on the amount leftover. By creating a business, you can control the

## Business Spending Cycle

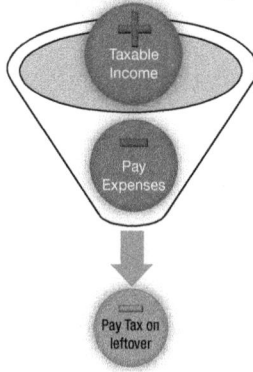

amount of money you spend on taxes. This is how Warren Buffet and millions of other wealthy Americans pay less tax per year than an employee earning a $60,000 salary!

### "Loopholes" is NOT a Dirty Word!

I speak all across the country teaching people how to use tax planning as a way to keep more of what they earn. When preparing for my media appearances, I always have to chuckle when a show producer instructs me not to use the word, "loopholes." There is a common misconception that someone using loopholes is a shady person, or someone practicing tax avoidance. The truth is that loopholes are created by the government. They want us to use loopholes. Loopholes are just government incentives to promote its public policy.

Most loopholes exist for business owners. More deductions, breaks, and credits exist for business owners because business is the heart of our economy. By providing breaks to businesses, our government can stimulate the economy and keep it flourishing in good times, and fuel it in recessions.

This is especially evident now, in our troubled economic times. We can clearly see Washington's stimulus geared to ward businesses because small business employs people, invests in equipment and capital resources, and creates general movement of cash in our economy. In a sense, providing breaks to businesses helps to jump-start our economy. Since the government wants our economy to grow, they design the majority of stimulus aid toward business to create a change in our economic climate.

I am one of this country's top experts in the art of paying less tax, but even the very best in tax planners can only do so much for an employee paying a lot of tax. In fact, as employees earn more in their paycheck, they actually *lose* deductions, credits, and loopholes! I propose then, if you want to make more money, you must change the WAY you earn your money. It is then that you will change *how much* you make by keeping more of what you earn. This concept is financial defense at its best and will help you take charge of your financial future.

Working under this strategy of converting "post-tax" dollars to "pre-tax" dollars, you can essentially use a business to provide ways to take your ordinary spending and make it tax deductible spending. How do you accomplish this? Start a business! And I should add, start the RIGHT business.

If the idea of starting a business intrigues you, lets start by identifying the steps to create your very own (legal) tax shelter. Don't wait, you can start today!

## What is a Legitimate Business?

The first step to starting a business, is to start! You may consider starting a part-time business initially as you continue to work in your full time employment. This can often be the smartest way to create tax benefits as you build your business with added tax savings as a bonus.

We are living in an age of convenience. This provides many opportunities for entrepreneurs to get started in business, in endless possibilities of activities. If you don't already have an idea for a business, evaluate your favorite activities. From a financial perspective, I recommend examining your spending habits. Where do you spend the most money? Is there a way to create a business around that activity?

I recently shared this discussion with a client, Ed, whose hobby was music. He was a faithful, devoted fan who spent most of his spare time attending concerts, meeting artists, and talking with other fans about his passion. This pursuit was clear in examining his financial records. Concert tickets, subscriptions, and music purchases were the source of much of his after tax dollars. After learning the powerful tax benefits of owning a business, the music industry was a natural option for Ed. Even without musical talent as a performer, there are many opportunities to use his expertise and skills in the area, and he went on to manage an up-and-coming rock band as a part-time business.

## Hobby Loss Rules

Unfortunately, it is not simply the action of <u>starting</u> business which enables you to take tax deductions for your after-tax dollars. Most personal time pursuits fall under what are known as the "Hobby Loss" rules, a special set of guidelines used by the IRS to eliminate your ability to deduct expenses for doing what makes you happy simply to avoid tax.

To prevent abuse of business loopholes, the IRS uses criteria to determine if, in fact, you have a hobby or a business. If you merely have a hobby, you are precluded from deducting losses related to that activity.

The beauty of incorporating a business into your tax plan however, lies in knowing the rules and structuring your business appropriately to follow the law. When you meet the IRS criteria for having a business, you can enjoy all the tax benefits that come along with your business including converting after-tax dollars into pre-tax dollars.

## IRS Hobby Loss Criteria

There is no question that the IRS will gladly accept, and in fact requires your payment of tax for income generated from your business. However, the grey areas of whether or not an activity is a business or a hobby matters most when there are losses. Your ability to deduct any losses from your business will help lower your current tax bill. Meeting these criteria will enable you to deduct any losses you experience in the business against other forms of your income.

First, you must carry-on the activity in a business-like manner with a for-profit motive. This is easy to accomplish and document in case you need to defend your position during an examination. Make sure you treat your business separate from your household financial activity. This means using a separate business bank account to receive your business income and pay your business expenses. Keep organized records of your business activity. Easy-to-use bookkeeping software like QuickBooks can help organize your business financial records.

You must be involved in your activity with the purpose of making a profit. This is truly what distinguishes a hobby from a true business. I also must emphasize the importance of the word profit. It is not enough just to create *income*, but profit is what is left over after all expenses have been paid to generate your income. You should be sure and document your intention and efforts to create profit in your business. Diaries, meeting minutes, copies of advertisements and marketing plans all can support your "for profit" motive.

If you've experienced losses in your business, you should show that losses are normal for your type of business. This can be as simple as citing profit statistics for early stage businesses in your industry. Additionally, you should document your attempt to improve profitability. Again diaries, meeting minutes and marketing plans can be beneficial for proving this criteria has been met.

You should be able to prove that you, or your advisors, have the knowledge needed to carry out the activity as a business. Curriculum vitae, references from previous colleagues, and certificates from continuing education classes can help support your position. If you have had similar successful businesses in the past, be sure to include records from these experiences.

It is helpful to demonstrate that the activity has made a profit in some years. This is not to say that if you never have a profit you are not legally entitled to deduct your losses. In fact, one recent court case featuring a farmer with 29 years of losses proved that you don't have to have a profit in order to prevail in deducting your losses. However, prior profits certainly help demonstrate the legitimacy of your activity as a business and not a hobby.

Finally, if you have a reasonable expectation of future profit, be sure and document this as well. This may be due to new marketing efforts, economic forecasts, or new revenue opportunities. Again, be sure to document these items to support your position.

## Choosing the RIGHT Business Structures for Maximum Tax Benefit

There are 3 basic types of businesses which include **sole proprietorships** (businesses with one owner), **partnerships** (businesses with more than one owner), and **corporations** (a separate legal entity governed by state law).

Of these types, there are many different business structures.

### SOLE PROPRIETORSHIPS

Most businesses start as a sole proprietorship. It is the easiest of all the entities to establish because it requires no paperwork! For this reason, it is the least expensive to operate; from an administrative standpoint that is! Sole proprietorships have certain advantages, but in general can create additional tax and audit risk. The majority of sole proprietorships I see may have been appropriate at the beginning of a business, but as the owner's needs change with time, they are no longer effective. As such, sole proprietorships, unless established for particular tax benefits, are generally not the most appropriate choice for tax planning.

# Sole Proprietorship

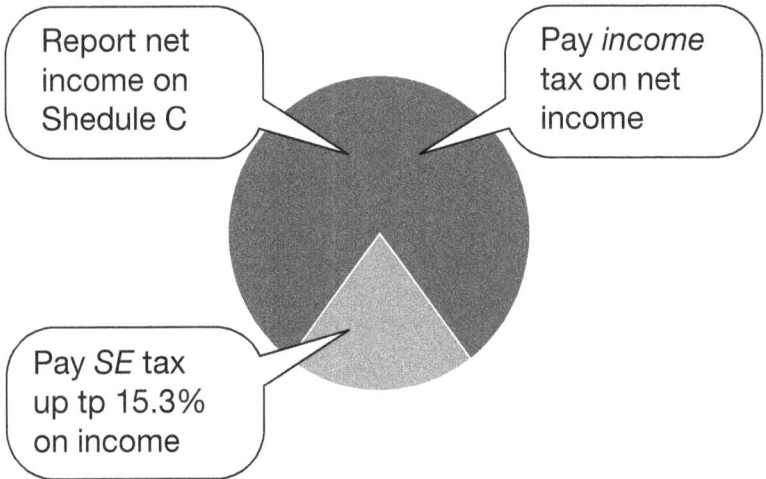

Report net income on Shedule C

Pay *income* tax on net income

Pay *SE* tax up tp 15.3% on income

If you operate your business as a sole proprietorship, you may pay as much in self-employment tax as you do in income tax. If you are taxed as a sole proprietor, you'll report your net income on Schedule C of your form 1040. In a sole proprietorship, you'll pay tax on your business profits at whatever your personal rate is. But you'll also pay self-employment tax, of 15.3% on your first $106,800** of "net self-employment income" and 2.9% of any-thing above that.

**Sole Proprietorship Landmines**
Self-employment tax on profits, no deductibility of fringe benefits, higher risk of audit

Let's say your profit at the end the year is $80,000. You'll pay regular tax at your regular rate, whatever that is. You'll also pay about $11,000 in self-employment tax. The self-employment tax replaces the Social Security and Medicare tax that your employer would pay and withhold if you weren't self-employed. Sole proprietorships do not pay a separate federal income tax. As illustrated above, the profits are reported on the owner's tax return and tax is paid at the rate of the individual owner.

*\*\*2010 Amounts*

## PARTNERSHIPS

If you have more than one person involved in the ownership of your business, you have a partnership. This is true even if you haven't formed a formal partnership agreement! Even a verbal agreement of doing business between 2 or more individuals creates a partnership.

Partnerships present some of the most complex areas of legal and tax law. As with sole proprietorships, partners in a partnership are subject to self-employment tax on the business profits. But

# Partnership

Report net income on Shedule E

Pay *income* tax on net income

Pay *SE* tax up tp 15.3% on income

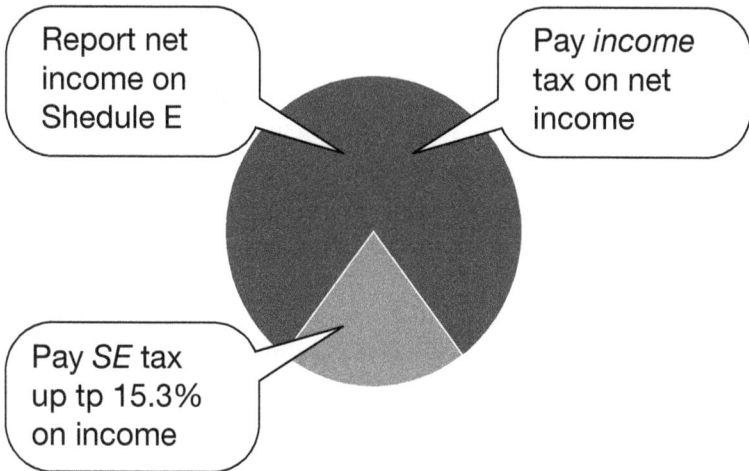

they can be an easy way to get started in a new business without the expense of forming another type of entity. Partnerships are known as "pass through" entities in that the profits and losses from the partnership "pass through" to the individual owners' tax returns. In turn, the individual owners pay tax at whatever their personal tax rate. As with sole proprietorships, partnerships do not pay

**Partnership Landmines**

Self-employment tax on profits, no deductibility of fringe benefits, specialty tax issues for adding and removing partners business federal income taxes on their profits. However, profits earned in a partnership generally are subject to self-employment tax. This sometimes can be more than the owner's federal income tax!

One convenient feature of a partnership is that partners can decide as often as they prefer how to share in profits and losses of the business. This provides great flexibility in tax planning. For example, if the business experiences losses and one particular partner can benefit from deducting the losses over another, they can simply agree to the special allocation and report these special allocations of income and deductions as they determine appropriate for the owners.

## S CORPORATION

A third type of business entity is the S corporation. An "S" corporation is a special corporation that's taxed like a partnership. The corporation pays you a reasonable wage for the work you do. If there's any profit left over, it passes through to you, and you pay the tax on that income on your own return. So the S corporation splits the owners income into two parts, wages and pass-through distributions.

Here is why the S corporation is so attractive. You will pay the same 15.3% tax on your wages as you would on your self-employment income. But – there's no Social Security or self-employment tax due on the dividend pass-through. Using this tax planning strategy, S corporation owners can create tax savings through a reduction of their self-employment tax.

**S Corporation Landmines**
Reasonable compensation audit issues, no deductibility of fringe benefits, no disproportionate distributions, loss basis issues

The S corporation, like a partnership, is a pass-through entity. Net profits are passed through to the individual shareholders, who each pay taxes on their share at their own individual rates. One restriction of the S corporation, however is that the owners

# S-Corporation

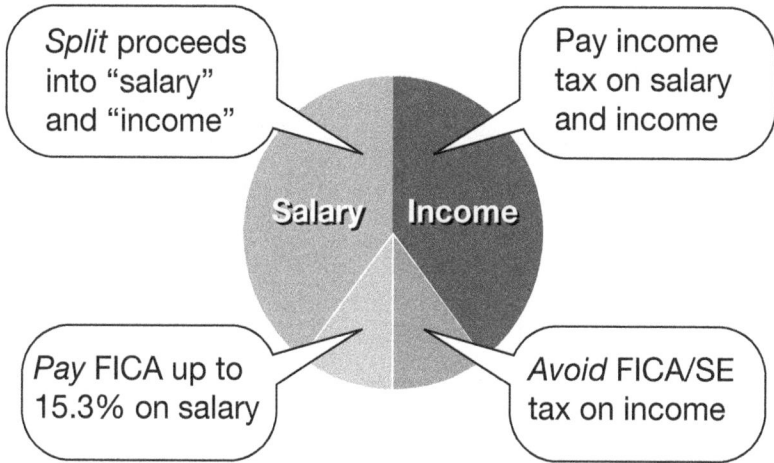

*Split* proceeds into "salary" and "income"

Pay income tax on salary and income

**Salary** | **Income**

*Pay* FICA up to 15.3% on salary

*Avoid* FICA/SE tax on income

cannot receive disproportionate distributions. This means that income and losses must be allocated to each shareholder according to his ownership percentage.

**CORPORATION**

A corporation is a separate legal entity governed by state law. C corporations must prepare and file their own tax returns and pay tax at special corporate tax rates. Sometimes these rates can be lower than the individual owner's tax rates, providing an opportunity for tax planning to take advantage of this rate difference. The corporate tax, however, can pose an additional tax because as these profits are distributed to the shareholders in the form of dividends, the owners pay tax on the dividends at their own individual rates. I've seen many C corporations who were unnecessarily paying this "double" tax on profits – first at the corporate level and then as the owners withdrew profits from the business. This is one of the major disad-

**Corporation Landmines**
Double tax issues, inability to "pass-through" losses to owners, specialty taxes *(accumulated earnings tax, personal holding company tax, personal service corp tax issues)*

# C Corporation

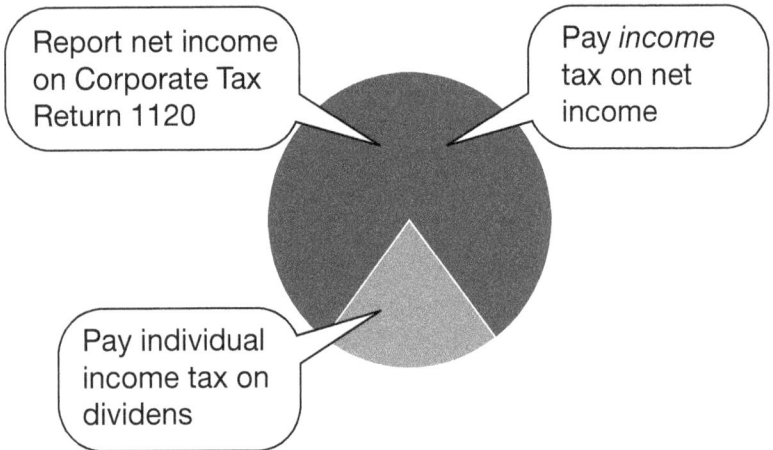

Report net income on Corporate Tax Return 1120

Pay *income* tax on net income

Pay individual income tax on dividens

vantages of owning a C corporation. C corporations have many wonderful tax benefits. They have the most deductions available of any business structure, including the ability to deduct valuable fringe benefits for the owners. C corporations are also great for growing businesses, businesses with plans to become publicly traded companies and in general, corporations with more than 100 shareholders.

## LLC

The LLC is a relatively young type of business structure which offers a hybrid between a partnership and an S corporation. It works much like a partnership or S corporation in that its profits pass-through to its individual owners. Yet unlike a partnership, the LLC contains powerful legal liability protection which can help protect its owners more than a partnership or even an S corporation.

The LLC is an extremely flexible entity structure which can be taxed many ways. For example, an LLC with a single member (1 owner) is considered a disregarded entity for fed eral tax purposes. For this reason, profits and losses from an LLC are reported on a taxpayer's Schedule C or Schedule E (for rental properties) of the owner's form 1040.

The LLC can also elect to be taxed as an S corporation. All the tax attributes I mentioned regarding S corporations would apply to an LLC which has elected S corporation tax treatment.

Finally, LLC's can also elect to be taxed as a C corporation. In this case, the LLC would file its own tax return, and pay taxes at corporate tax rates for its profits.

**LLC Landmines**

Most LLC owners make no election for how their business will be taxed. By default, an LLC is taxed either as a sole proprietorship or a partnership and receive all the disadvantages included with those entity structures.

Business owners who choose to hold their business or investments inside of an LLC, generally do so to take advantage of the valuable liability protection laws governing this type of business structure. However, they can still maintain this liability protection while maximizing their tax benefits by making the proper tax elections for the entity.

## Selecting the RIGHT Entity to Minimize Your Tax

You'll notice that each entity I've discussed above, has its own set of legal and tax advantages. Yet most business owners approach the decision of which business is right for them by consulting with an attorney. Their decision-making process, therefore, focuses on the legal benefits and nuances surrounding the entity choice. The side effect to approaching your business decision this way, is that you can often miss valuable tax breaks available. This happens so frequently in fact, that when I'm meeting with a new client for the first time, most have no understanding of why they are holding their business in a particular entity structure. And most have no idea that operating as a different entity can have monumental tax consequences.

The first thing to consider when you're trying to decide which type of business structure will work best for you, is to decide which one will be most beneficial to your tax plan. The bottom line question you should ask yourself is, "What pre-tax spending will your business structure provide you, and is this the area which will benefit you most?"

Look at your spending patterns. Where do you spend the most money? Does the business entity you are considering provide a tax advantage for this type of expense?

At the end of the day, if you're serious about getting your business to succeed, and you want to make the most of your tax plan, you're going to need some help. Nobody can be an expert at everything, and the tax code is complicated. Enlisting the help of a tax planning specialist can also provide support for the IRS Hobby Loss criteria. Make sure you work with someone who not only has good knowledge of the tax code and filing requirements, but who will work with you proactively throughout the year to make sure you are taking advantage of every available break. Do not limit yourself to working with someone face-to-face. Modern technology provides many opportunities to work with the RIGHT advisor, even if that person is across the country, instead of across the street.

## About Dominique

Dominique Molina, CPA CTC
President
American Institute of Certified Tax Coaches
CertifiedTaxCoach.com
CertifiedTaxCoach.org

Dominique Molina is the co-founder and President of the American Institute of Certified Tax Coaches. As the driving force and visionary behind the San Diego-based company, Ms. Molina set out to change the way tax professionals approach tax planning. In 2009, Ms. Molina began to create an elite network of tax professionals including CPAs, EAs, attorneys and financial service providers who are trained to help their clients proactively plan and implement tax strategies that can rescue thousands of dollars in wasted tax. Her more than 12 years of hands-on experience in the accounting and business fields provide her with ample skills to accomplish this mission. Ms. Molina has successfully licensed tax professionals as Certified Tax Coaches across the country, creating a national network of highly qualified advisors. This premier group of professionals features less than 200 specialists in 40 states who have achieved this very specialized designation.

Prior to founding Certified Tax Coach, Ms. Molina successfully managed her own practice, AccountOnIt, a San Diego-based, full-service tax, accounting, and business consulting firm, serving hundreds of business owners and investors across the country for seven years. Preceding this, Ms. Molina assisted a variety of clients for the largest independently-owned CPA firm in San Diego.

Ms. Molina received her bachelor's degree in Accounting from San Diego State University. Upon graduation, she began her accounting work as a staff accountant, controller, and office manager at several closely-held asset management and investment companies.

Ms. Molina frequently appears as a tax expert and TV guest in regional television markets. Her excellent media credentials, professionalism, and outgoing personality allow her to provide expert advice on tax issues for thousands of Americans. Ms. Molina is also a published author of two books on taxation, and has written one of our country's preeminent tax planning textbooks. A frequent lecturer and speaker, Ms. Molina often teaches at professional association conferences for tax accountants, and instructs continuing professional education courses for various organizations. Her website also receives thousands of visitors per month who follow her financial video blogs.

When not solving the challenges of America's taxpayers, Ms. Molina loves being a wife and a mother. She spends her free time with her family enjoying San Diego, surfing, tennis, reading, traveling and running. Ms. Molina is also a classical pianist.

If you're wondering if YOU pay too much in tax, visit www.CertifiedTaxCoach. com to take our free tax mistakes quiz.

# CHAPTER 12

# Breaking The Tax Code
## – EAT, DRINK, BE MERRY
## – AND DOCUMENT, DOCUMENT, DOCUMENT

By Gary D. Heldt, Jr., CPA

*"You must pay taxes. But there's no law that says you gotta leave a tip."*
~ Morgan Stanley advertisement

If you own your own business, you understand that there are times where it's absolutely essential to wine and dine clients – and even entertain your own employees with a summer picnic or holiday party.

Believe it or not, the IRS understands that too. They know that sometimes, a critical part of doing business is *not* to do business – and to instead entertain important customers by taking them to a basketball game or some other event.

Unfortunately, there's something else the IRS knows – and that's the fact that the Meals and Entertainment business deduction is one of the most widely abused deductions on tax returns.

That's why the Meals and Entertainment deduction has some of the most stringent rules and regulations regarding what's allowable and what's not. And also why you're only allowed to deduct

50% of them in most cases.

Yes, I said "most." Many taxpayers are unaware that there are certain instances where you can actually write off the entire cost of a meal or party provided to employees or clients.

When you plan accordingly and set up your events, entertainment and meals to be as IRS-friendly as possible, you can save a lot on your taxes – *and* have a good time. In this chapter, we're going to talk about how to maximize your Meal and Entertainment deductions and also about how to make sure your M&E deductions are as "audit-proof" as possible.

## AN M&E CASE STUDY

When you *don't* make the effort to protect your M&E deductions from an audit, you could be in for a lot of grief – and possibly a lot of extra taxes.

I can illustrate just that scenario by relating the story of a client who was referred to me for help. He was a real estate broker who was in the midst of a large-scale audit. The IRS auditor was very severe – and was threatening to disallow ALL of his M&E deductions, which were very large. If that happened, my new client was going to owe the IRS an extra $30,000 – not a happy prospect.

The big problem the real estate broker had was the lack of proper documentation. While he had receipts from most of his M&E expenses and was able to get the ones he was missing from credit card statements, he did not keep track of the business purpose of the expenses, where they occurred or the names of the clients he was entertaining.

The IRS requires that this basic information ("who, where and why") be kept either in a log or written on the back of the receipts in question. They also require it be recorded in a timely manner – if you can't do it within 24 hours of the M&E expense, then it at least has to be recorded in a weekly log.

That meant, technically, my new client couldn't regroup and simply try to supply that information from memory.

Fortunately, what he *did* have was an appointment book, with the "who," "where" and sometimes even the "why" already written down for most of the M&E expenses. And these appointments were obviously recorded close to the actual events in question, so they passed the "timely manner" test.

We used the appointment book and all the receipts to then put together an "entertainment book" for the auditor, with complete documentation of all the deductions that the broker listed on his tax return.

But the auditor, who was a little green, still fought us on many issues.

For example, because the broker represented many properties, he would invite other real estate agents over to his house and present a slide show of the properties to them. By doing this at home, rather than holding individual open houses at the actual properties, he saved a lot of time and money. Naturally, he would serve the agents some food and drink at the slide show at his home.

The auditor felt like he was trying to get away with charging off parties at his house that weren't business-related. Fortunately, the broker had the slide shows in question, photos of the agents at the slide shows, the guest lists for these events and the receipts for the food and beverage. The auditor had to allow the deduction, as we simply had too much proof that it was business-oriented.

The broker also held a large holiday party at his home, where he invited everyone that had bought a home from him or had referred new clients during the past year. Again, the auditor thought it was a personal party that the IRS didn't really have to cover. Again, the broker had substantial evidence that it was all about business, including a copy of the actual invitation that was sent to clients which specifically indicated it was a business gathering. The auditor ended up allowing that deduction as well.

Finally, the broker had also deducted expenses for playing golf with clients as well as taking them to football games – he had season tickets for one team. The auditor also tried to say they weren't relevant to his business. However, the IRS guidelines specifically state that you are allowed to entertain a client in this manner as long as you discuss business before the entertainment takes place. In all cases, the broker entertained these clients after business meetings – he had all the meetings documented in his appointment book – so the deductions were allowed.

Well, *almost* all of them. The broker wanted to deduct the entire cost of the season football tickets. The auditor ruled (and rightly so) that the broker had to break down the cost of the tickets per individual game – and could only write off the games he used to entertain business clients. The end result of all this work? My client the real estate broker now only owed the IRS $5000 after the audit, instead of $30,000 – which he could live with.

## Helping Businesses Find Their Tax Advantage

You can see from the above story just how important it is to have the right person behind you when you face a situation with the IRS.

Although we provide a wide range of financial, accounting and tax services to our clients, nothing pleases me more than personally helping a client like that real estate broker, and providing the best service possible at the fairest possible price. It's why I became an accountant in the first place. My mom was a single parent and schoolteacher who raised me and my two sisters on her own. When I was in high school, she was finally able to buy a house. Because of this new and potentially complex financial situation, she thought it best to have her taxes done by a professional for that first year of home ownership, instead of doing the return on her own as she had in previous years.

When I found out the accountant she hired had charged her $350 (and this was a few years ago, remember) for what was still a relatively simple tax return, I was outraged and was sure she had been taken advantage of. And I decided then and there to go to school, learn accounting and not take advantage of people who hired me.

The next day, I signed up for bookkeeping class. I got a lot of looks, being 6'3" and a football player – not the usual candidate for accounting. But it was amazing – I took to it like a duck to water. It was almost second nature to me.

After my education, I worked for both for-profit companies and nonprofits, learning the ropes. My goal was to gain a wide range of experience so I could work with all kinds of businesses when I went on my own.

That happened in 1999, when I bought an existing accounting practice. We started with 140 personal tax clients and 75 business clients. Since then, we've built those numbers up to about 775 personal and 200 business clients. And we did it all through word-of-mouth. Up until last year, we did no advertising or marketing of any kind.

One of the secrets of our success is that we have a very strong, secure website that our clients can access 24/7. They can upload their documents through a secure portal, or download information and work we've completed for them as well. This allows us to work with clients all over the country and even all over the world. We have many clients in the military – some even sending us their tax information from a submarine somewhere in the Pacific.

We also work hard at maintaining a close relationship with our clients. In addition to checking in with them regularly, we also put out a monthly newsletter, that features a column written by my son, Tyler. Actually, since *"Tyler's Corner"* began when he was a newborn, he doesn't really write it…but some of our clients have threatened to fire us if we ever stop printing it! I don't think they'd really leave us, but you never know…

Finally, we think it's important to give back to the community. We formed a business referral group in our area – where trusted firms can recommend each other when clients need a different product or service to what our individual companies offer. We also founded a nonprofit charity called *"For the Kids."* For the past 11 years, *For the Kids* has organized a charity golf tournament where we raise money for a seriously ill child. In 2010, we were fortunate enough to be able to donate over $21,000 to a local family in need of the money for medical bills.

I believe there is a certain level of service you should be able to expect from anyone that you hire to do your tax planning – and I make sure to provide that same level to my clients. Here are three things to look for:

**1. The top person at the firm should be available to you.**

I make myself available to any of our clients if they really need to talk to me; I don't hide in my office. I believe in service to the point where we *underpromise* and *overdeliver*. That's how I would've liked my mom to be treated.

**2. Your accountant should contact you for regular updates.**

We try to connect with all our clients on a monthly basis so we know what's going on with their finances and how they might want to handle things for their next tax return.

**3. Your accountant should be helping you plan in advance for the next tax year.**

If you plan now, you can often plot out significant tax advantages by how you approach your finances. If you wait until it's April 15th, you're generally stuck with what you've done and there's not as much you can do to lower your taxes.

## M&E Tax Tips

The kind of planning I just spoke about really can help you save when it comes to Meals & Entertainment deductions. I'd like to close out this chapter with a few more tax tips on this deduction that you may not be aware of:

- If you give someone tickets to an event, it's better to take that as an entertainment deduction rather than a business gift deduction. That's because you can only write off $25 for any business gift, no matter what the actual cost.

- You *can* deduct the cost of entertaining your spouse and children in certain instances. The general rule of thumb is, if the client or business associate you're entertaining has their spouse and kids with them, it's reasonable for you to bring yours.

- You can deduct the cost of providing lunches for your staff – depending again on certain criteria. The tax code says if your employees have 45 minutes or less for their lunch break and there aren't enough eating establishments in the immediate area, this is allowable. But you must supply lunches for at least over half of the staff.

When you do supply meals to employees under the above conditions, you can deduct 100% of the cost, instead of just 50%. Here are a few more instances where that's the case:

## TICKETS TO A CHARITABLE SPORTS EVENT
Remember that charity golf tournament that our nonprofit company holds every year earlier? Well, if you brought a client to it, the cost of the tickets would be 100% deductible.

## FOOD AT THE OFFICE
The IRS allows employers to deduct 100% of the expense of stocking the office kitchen for employees. Coffee, soft drinks, and other snacks and beverages bought to be consumed on the business premises all qualify.

## EMPLOYEE PARTIES
Whether it's a holiday party, a summer office barbeque or a company awards banquet, it's 100% deductible – as are all recreational, social and/or entertainment gatherings that are primarily for the benefit of *all* employees – *not* just the executive suite!

**MEALS FOR THE PUBLIC**

Maybe, to promote your new Jiffy Lube, you decide to give away free hot dogs on a Saturday afternoon. Those dogs (and all the trimmings) are 100% deductible – as is any food you give away to whoever shows up. The trick here is that they are actually considered *advertising* expenses.

**FOOD AND BEVERAGE FOR A SALES SEMINAR**

If you hold a sales seminar, and you have snacks and drinks for the attendees, the cost again is 100% deductible. That's because they come under the cost of the actual seminar and are not considered part of the Meals & Entertainment deduction.

## Conclusion – Documentation and Planning

Remember always to document the "who, what and where" of M&E expenses. You also don't need to hold on to receipts for less than $75, but you should note the expense in a log, along with the necessary business substantiation.

Lastly, always keep up to date with the latest IRS regulations. Changes to the tax code are made frequently by Congress, so consult with your tax professional or accountant – so you can do your tax planning with the correct information.

When you adhere to the IRS regulations and do the necessary documentation, you can enjoy a big Meals & Entertainment deduction without having to sweat the threat of an audit. After all, Meals & Entertainment should be the fun part of running a business – so enjoy yourself and enjoy saving on your tax bill!

## About Gary

Gary D. Heldt, Jr., is a Certified Public Accountant. Gary owns and operates **Small Business Advisors**, in Gambrills, Maryland. Small Business Advisors serves a client base from the Baltimore, MD, Washington, DC and Northern Virginia vicinity, and holds the title of Premier Tax Coach in Anne Arundel County, Maryland.

Gary acquired Small Business Advisors in 1999. Prior to that, however, and subsequent to his graduation from Shepherd College, and with an Accounting education under his belt, Gary's focus was to gain a wide range of experience with his Accounting knowledge, working in both the for-profit and non-profit industries. This foundation within these industries, combined with the desire to provide the best service possible at the fairest possible price, led Gary to open his own business doing just that in 1999.

Since 1999, Gary has grown Small Business Advisors by five times its acquired size, and maintained a retention rate of 94% while doing so. A majority of this growth was through word-of-mouth. Up until last year, there was no advertising or marketing of any kind. Maintaining a close relationship with clients, including checking in with them regularly, resulted in this successful growth.

Gary's clients rely upon his competent and experienced advice. Gary's clients receive total financial services, whether they are individuals, large or small businesses, or other types of businesses and agencies. Gary is dedicated to the three underlying principles of professionalism, responsiveness and quality. Gary's reputation for providing quality service reflects the high standards he demands of himself. His high standards, responsive service and specialized staff, spell the difference between Small Business Advisors and "the rest".

Gary also believes that it is important to give back to the community. He helped form a business referral group where trusted firms recommend each other when their own clients need a different product or service that they themselves cannot provide. Gary and Small Business Advisors also helped found a non-profit charity called *"For The Kids"*, and for the past 11 years, this charity has organized a charity golf tournament where funds are raised for seriously ill children. In 2010 alone, the charity was fortunate enough to be able to donate over $21,000 to a local family in need of money for medical bills.

Gary Heldt, Jr., CPA and Small Business Advisors are more than "just Accountants".

## CHAPTER 13

# How to DECREASE Your Business taxes by THOU$ANDS with one simple change

### By Gina Weller, ABA, ATP, CEC
### Owner, Weller Consulting

**D**o you have an entrepreneurial spirit? Does the thought of starting your own business excite you? Do you wake up every morning grateful that "you" are the boss?

Few things in life elicit the same thrill for an entrepreneur more than knowing they can get up every day, do what they are passionate about, and actually get paid to do it! This hardly seems like work, does it?

It is so easy for that "free spirit" to get so caught up in enjoying the dream of their business, that they sometimes don't spend much time thinking about, researching, or implementing the most important aspect of the start-up process – choosing and forming the proper legal entity with which to operate their business.

Getting proper guidance and help with this decision in the beginning is crucial, and can save you money, time, and unnecessary headaches in the long run. The key word in that last sentence is **proper** guidance, not just guidance about what your choices are.

Would it pique your interest if I told you that this one seemingly unimportant decision could be the very decision that allows you to put **THOUSANDS** more into your pocket each year in spendable cash through tax savings? I don't know about you, but I sure would rather see **THOUSANDS** more in my bank account each year than in Uncle Sam's!

What? ... putting **THOUSANDS** more in your pocket each year with tax savings? Let's explore this concept deeper by comparing two local business owners and competitors. We will call them Harry* and Stan*. Harry got some great advice in the beginning stages of setting up his business from an advisor. He was advised on which entity choice was right for him and his business, and which would save him the most in taxes each year. Stan, on the other hand, decided to use the internet to explore his business entity options. He decided to go with the easiest and cheapest route without getting any further advice. He decided he would just revisit this in a few years if his business actually took off. Let's see how each is doing after two years in business.

Harry works hard as do most business owners, but he also enjoys being able to take advantage of the perks and freedoms his business allows him. His advisor educated him on his choices of entity structures he could choose from, while tying it all together with many legal business deductions and business strategies that Harry never knew existed.

Implementing the proper legal structure, deductions and strategies into his business has saved Harry a minimum of $20,000 per year in taxes, when compared to Stan. With these tax savings, Harry was able to take his entire family on a cruise to the Bahamas this summer, and came back with an awesome tan. He also just bought himself a new SUV to go with that tan and is sporting it around town now with his new business sign on the door. Harry can't wait to visit his advisor next quarter to see how much money he is going to save on his taxes this year. He is already thinking about what he is going to do with the extra money. Ahh... life is good...

*Harry and Stan are fictitious characters. Any resemblance to 'real life' clients is strictly coincidental.*

Stan also works hard, but is really troubled by his tax bill, which rose significantly this past year when he went in to get his taxes done. Stan now dreads to see April 15th coming each year, because he knows he will be writing out a big check payable to the Internal Revenue Service. This year, when Stan wrote out that check, he couldn't quite remember the reason he decided to go into business in the first place.

Stan feels like no matter what he does or how hard he works, he just never can seem to get ahead. To him it seems like the more money he makes in his business, the less money he has to spend on himself. If that wasn't enough, Stan had a customer threaten to sue him the other day if he didn't take care of an issue that the customer claimed his employees caused. Stan is now wondering if he is going to be held personally liable if the customer decides to follow through with his threat to sue.

Stan is perplexed. He really can't figure out how Harry, his competitor down the street, can afford to be driving around town in that new SUV promoting his business with a smile on his face, and how in the world does he have time to take off for a vacation to get that tan? Stan can't remember the last vacation he took. He knows that Harry isn't getting any more business than he is, but there is definitely something different in the way their businesses look and operate. Stan thinks to himself ... "What am I missing?"

At first glance, it may appear that Harry is better at promoting and providing services in his business than Stan, and that is why he has more spendable cash each year from his business. While this could be one reason Harry has more money to spend each year, in this case it isn't. They both have a business with similar income and service levels, and Stan and Harry are both quite knowledgeable in their chosen trades. The reason Harry manages to end his year with more spendable cash in his business than Stan is because Harry spent the time necessary when setting up his business to get guidance on the parts of his business about which he wasn't so knowledgeable. He has a properly setup entity structure which serves him well, protects him personally, and helps him put about $20,000 more per year in spendable cash in his pocket than Stan, due to tax savings.

Fortunately for Stan and many other current business owners in Stan's position, help IS available. The original choice of entity when a business is started is not usually a decision which cannot be changed, regardless of the age of the business.

With proper guidance and advice, even Stan can turn his business around and start feeling the joy of spending or saving an additional $20,000 each year, instead of sending it to the Internal Revenue Service. Then he will again remember why he decided to go into business for himself. Having your own business can truly be the American dream. Not getting the proper advice can turn it into the American nightmare! It is this very scenario that drove me to open my practice back in 2001.

After graduating college and working for businesses both large and small as an accountant for about 7 years, I knew that at some point I wanted to be in business for myself. At that time, I just wasn't sure how that was all going to evolve. Well, as luck would have it, I seemed to be at the right place at the right time and had the opportunity to learn a new skill. That skill, coupled with my current accounting knowledge, would allow me to branch out after a year on my own as a freelance business consultant. I specialized in software implementation in the area of finance and tax for large businesses.

What I found out really quickly was that I was now a 1099 contractor instead of a W2 employee as I always had been, and the tax issue became a huge part of my life that first year. Signs of the American nightmare had started for me.

When my tax liability approached an astounding high five figures that first year, I knew that there had to be something more I could do to control this. What I remember seeing when I started reading tax articles were headlines such as "secrets of the rich", or "secrets the IRS doesn't want you know about." This convinced me that I must be missing a piece to this puzzle, so I spent the better part of the next 7 years studying anything and everything I could possibly get my hands on that would help save on my taxes – including Internal Revenue Service Publications and Code.

Through my studies, it lead me to change my businesses legal structure, use multiple entity strategies at times to shift income to lower tax brackets, and start to use a host of other deductions and loopholes the Internal Revenue Service had created yet most tax advisors were not talking about. It all became somewhat of a game to me to see how much income I could earn, and how low I could legally drop my tax bracket each year. I became very excited about all that I was learning and would often share my newest-found strategy with anyone who would listen.

In 2001, I decided to open up a practice where I could spend my time focused on helping both individuals and business owners save as much on their taxes as legally possible. This has been and still remains my passion in life today.

I love to speak with people who are thinking of opening a business and hear the passion in their voice about what it is they want to do in their new business – and be able to know that I can help them fulfill that dream with the best advice possible on the entity structure, tax strategies and liability protection they can put into place.

Working with current business owners, and showing them how to put more money in their pockets through the appropriate legal entity, as well as by using tax strategies they had no idea existed, is just as rewarding to me as it is to the business owner.

Following is a list of the types of the most common business entities available, along with some brief information about each type. It is by no means meant to be an all-inclusive list, and should not be used as the only information from which you use to decide which entity is best for you.

- Sole Proprietorship – an unincorporated form of business with one owner. It is not a separate legal entity from its owner and provides very little, if any, liability protection to the owner. For tax purposes, all income and expense of the business are reported on the personal return of the owner on a Schedule C. In addition to income taxes due on the net profit of the business, the sole proprietor is also subject to self-employment taxes (Social Security & Medicare) which is currently at 15.3%.

- Partnerships – there are two types of partnerships. General and Limited. A General partnership does not require any formal registration with a state, while the Limited partnership requires the filing of a certificate in the state in which you choose to operate. Partnerships are legal entities separate from their owners, and may or may not provide liability protection for the owners – depending on whether the owner is a general or limited partner. For tax purposes, partnerships do not pay taxes, and net income passes through to the partners personal returns. Taxes are paid by each partner on their share of income at their current tax rate. Partners may or may not be subject to self-employment taxes depending upon each partner's situation.

- Corporations – are separate legal entities from the owners or shareholders, and require registration in the state in which you choose to operate. They provide the shareholders with liability protection. For tax purposes, there are two taxation types for corporations. They can be taxed as a 'C' Corporation or an 'S' Corporation. A 'C' Corporation pays taxes at the business level and then money is distributed to the shareholders and may be taxed again at the shareholder level. An 'S' Corporation does not pay taxes at the business level, but passes the net income of the corporation to the shareholders personal return, and taxes are paid by each shareholder on their share of income at their current tax rate.

- Limited Liability Company (LLC) – is a legal entity separate from the members and requires registration in the state in which you choose to operate. They provide the members with liability protection. For tax purposes, an LLC can be taxed as a sole proprietor for single member LLCs, as a partnership for LLCs with two or more members, or as an 'S' or 'C' Corporation.

While there are a relatively small number of entity types from which you can choose, the legal details underlying each type can be inherently complex. It is always best to seek advice from a knowledgeable tax advisor who can look at your overall situation to help you determine which entity is best for you. The small investment you would have to make to hire a competent advisor could save you thousands in the future.

There are three major variables which a wise business advisor should use to help you determine which option is right for you. These variables are business control, owner liability and tax implication. If an advisor is not able to discuss all three variables with you in your decision process, then find another advisor!

As a purchaser of this book, I know that you are committed to finding out as much as you can about how to keep more money in your pocket through tax savings. If you are a current business owner or if you are thinking of starting a business, I am offering to you a special **FREE** gift which you can claim at www.wellerconsulting.com/taxcodeoffer.php. This URL is only available to owners and readers of this book.

I know that I am truly blessed to be able to share my passion and knowledge every day with those who need and want my help. It is an awesome feeling to know that I can touch so many lives and make them better – with the knowledge I will pass along.

I look forward to meeting each and every one of you who are ready to move your business to the next level, or those of you who have a business dream in your heart.

For more information or to schedule a consultation, please feel free to visit my website at: www.wellerconsulting.com, email me at: gina@wellerconsulting.com or call my office at 888-327-9306.

Don't forget to claim your FREE gift at: www.wellerconsulting.com/taxcodeoffer.php.

## About Gina

Gina Weller is the Owner of Weller Consulting, a tax, accounting and business consulting firm which offers "outside the box" solutions for their clients.

Gina has over 22 years of experience in a wide range of business environments. She has worked with both big and small businesses as well as public and private.

She has built her business around the principle of educating and helping others. Her diverse knowledge and experience allows her to bring new and innovative ideas to her clients.

When you bring Gina onto your team, you can feel confident that you are partnering with a professional who is honest and reliable and who will always have your best interest in mind.

Gina lives in Alpharetta, Georgia with her husband James, their son Garrett, and Missy their yellow lab.

You can contact Gina by phone at: 888-327-9306
or by email at: gina@wellerconsulting.com.

# CHAPTER 14

# Tax Planning

## By Larisa Humphrey

### ARE YOU PLANNING TO FAIL?

Let me start by dispelling the common misconception that tax planning only helps multi-billion dollar companies – big business. This is just not true. In fact, it's the small business owner who benefits most from tax planning, often reducing their taxable income to $0. With proper planning, small businesses can operate tax free!

Tax planning is finding legal ways to minimize your income taxes and protect your assets. The process consists of a comprehensive review of your business and personal financial affairs, then implementing strategies to keep more money in your pocket. The plan tells you what to do to cut your tax bill as much as possible and how to do it.

This includes tactics like deducting the family's medical expenses as a business deduction, writing off your children's allowance or private school tuition and structuring your business to avoid self employment tax. The tax code is stuffed with thousands of ways to reduce your taxes, but you must have a plan.

The key to a successful tax plan is all in the preparation. You must establish each program by IRS guidelines in advance. This is not something that can be done when you file your taxes after the tax year in question is over.

You'll need an up-to-date working knowledge of the ever-changing tax laws in order to formulate strategies that will stand up to an IRS audit. I recommend you see an experienced tax professional who is proficient in tax planning and stays current on tax law changes.

In my 20 years of tax preparation, I have seen countless clients who were very excited to report they started a new business during the year and made lots of money, only to find out they owed much of their profit to the federal and state governments.

They kick, scream and fight about how unfair the tax laws are and act like Uncle Sam was punishing them for starting a business. But if you don't have a plan for income taxes, you plan to fail.

A prime example would be my clients, a married couple, let's call them the TaxSavers. They run a multi-level marketing business that has grossed around $500,000 for the past couple of years.

They learned how to operate their business effectively and became experts at recruiting new associates. They sell a great deal of the company's products and make commission not only on the products they sell, but also on the products sold by associates in their downline. The TaxSavers do a great job running their business, but failed to protect their assets and their family's future. They didn't plan for income taxes. They planned to fail.

For the past three years, the TaxSavers have owed Uncle Sam somewhere between $55,000- $75,000, depending on how well they've kept track of their expenses—which usually isn't very well. Had they kept better records, I'm sure their tax bill would have been lower. But since the TaxSavers couldn't prove many of their expenses, simply because they paid cash, didn't keep receipts or both, they were stuck with enormous tax bills each year.

> **Note: Please see a professional bookkeeper/accountant to have your bookkeeping done.** It is well worth the cost! There is much more to bookkeeping than just data entry. In addition to keeping accurate, detailed records and providing you with reports that help you make better business decisions, a good bookkeeper is able to analyze your financial situation and give you important information that can save you a great deal of money. For instance, I had one client that didn't realize he was spending over $400 every month in ATM fees! (That's $4800 a year wasted!) Several other clients learned they could buy in bulk to save money since they were using more supplies than anticipated.

It boggles my mind how the TaxSavers continued to subject themselves to extremely high tax bills year after year, without making an effort to find a solution. Because of the way they operate their business, I knew the TaxSavers could turn many of their personal expenses into business tax deductions.

Following are the basic areas every business owner should examine when searching for tax-reducing programs. These basic strategies were sufficient for the TaxSavers because their income was only $500,000. The more income you have, the more complicated your tax plan will be.

**Top 10 Tax Planning Areas**
1. Entity Choice
2. Office space
3. Automobiles
4. Pay Yourself
5. Pay Your Family
6. Medical Expenses
7. Retirement Plan
8. Equipment/Furniture Rental
9. Daycare
10. Athletic Facility

## 1) ENTITY CHOICE: Is it costing you more?

The TaxSavers were operating their business as a sole pro-prietorship by default, since they did not bother to form any other business entity. **A sole proprietorship is <u>THE ABSO-LUTE WORST</u> business entity!**

(a) It provides absolutely no legal protection–- if someone sues you and wins, they can take everything you have worked so hard for, including your house, cars & your baby's sippy cup!

(b) Any profit from a sole proprietorship is subject to an addi-tional 15% self-employment tax that could be avoided sim-ply by choosing a different entity. The TaxSavers were pay-ing **UNNECESSARY TAXES!** Why would you pay tax that you don't have to pay? A supreme court justice (Judge Learned Hand) said "anyone may arrange his affairs so that his taxes shall be as low as possible; he is not bound to choose that pattern which best pays the treasury. There is not even a patriotic duty to increase one's taxes."

(c) In addition and most importantly, the tax form used for a sole proprietorship–schedule C–is **the most audited form at the IRS**. Just because you have a schedule C, the IRS is looking at your return a little closer. Believe me, you really don't want that! This reason alone should convince you to stop being a sole proprietor.

Mr. TaxSaver receives a 1099-Miscellaneous form from the main company every year for around $500,000. Zero taxes have been paid on this money and it is charged to Mr. TaxSaver's social security number.

My recommendation was to form two (2) corporations. The first one would be designated as an S-corporation for Mr. TaxSaver since he receives the 1099-M for $500,000. An S-corporation is not subjected to the additional 15% tax on profits (self employment tax) that a sole propri-etorship pays. So right off the bat, we are saving 15%

taxes on the business' annual profit!

I recommended a C corporation for Mrs. TaxSaver because she has long dreamed of owning her own catering service. Since the main business hosts several weekly meetings in the TaxSaver's home to recruit new business associates, it is the perfect opportunity for Mrs. TaxSaver to showcase her culinary skills by providing refreshments for the meetings. Mrs. TaxSaver hopes the meetings will be a source of catering leads. But in the meantime, the C-corporation serves a tri-fold purpose in tax planning: (a) by creating a deduction for the main company— payment for catering services rendered, (b) a vehicle through which she can hire their children and (c) an entity that can support a Medical Expense Reimbursement Plan. (Stay tuned...this will be explained later.)

**2) OFFICE SPACE:** The TaxSavers operate their business out of their home. I recommended they use their basement as office space. This would give them a hefty deduction for office space since they would depreciate 1/3 of their $700,000 home on their taxes every year. The corporation will pay the TaxSavers rent in the amount of $2500/mo, the going rate in their area for a space that size. This generates a deduction of $30,000 a year! (Note: The TaxSavers must claim this amount as rental income on their personal taxes, but against it they will write off expenses for 1/3 of the house, including mortgage, utilities, property taxes, repairs, etc.)

**3) AUTOMOBILE:** Both Mr. & Mrs. TaxSaver do a great deal of driving. They set up and attend numerous meetings to recruit new members 4-7 evenings a week. They estimate driving at least 100 miles each day. My recommendation is to set up an accountable plan which serves a 2-fold purpose: It reimburses them for mileage at the current mileage rate— 2010 rate is 50 cents per mile—which is TAX FREE money (meaning they don't have to report it on their taxes) and it gives the corporation a deduction of $18,250.

**4) PAY YOURSELF:** One of the biggest mistakes new business owners make is thinking they don't have to pay themselves a salary. They think it's ok to take money out of the business account to pay their personal expenses. They also think are avoiding the self employment tax. (This is the payroll tax you would have paid had received a W-2.) Well believe me, you aren't getting away with anything. The IRS has already decided what business owners who do what you do should make, and if you are audited, they will assess you that amount and charge you the payroll taxes, late fees, penalties and interest for not paying in a timely manner. Because of their specific duties in the business, I recommended Mr. TaxSaver take a salary of $85,000 and Mrs. TaxSaver take a salary of $55,000.

**5) PAY YOUR FAMILY:** The TaxSavers don't give their kids allowance anymore, they pay salaries and write it off on their taxes! They have a son in college and a daughter in private school – who both help host the 3-5 business meetings held in their home each week. The kids prepare and serve food, run the projector, pass out product samples and clean up after the affair. I recommended a salary of $300/week for each of them – which is $15,600/year. The TaxSavers are happy to get a tax deduction of $31,200 for the money they were giving their kids anyway. (Tax court has upheld that children as young as age 7 can work! Just be sure to keep time sheets, record duties and I recommend signing an employment agreement as well.)

Another benefit is the college-age child now qualifies for financial aid as an independent student. The TaxSavers no longer claim him as a dependent on their taxes, he files his own tax return. When the TaxSavers were claiming him as a dependent, he did not receive any financial aid because the TaxSaver's income was so high. But as an independent student, he is now receiving financial aid benefits.

The daughter in private school uses her salary to pay her $1000/month tuition – while the remainder is split between a Roth IRA which will be used for college tuition, her savings account and her pocket for spending money.

The TaxSavers also have a 14-year-old who built and hosts their website. He also maintains their email marketing and customer retention programs. I recommended a salary of $400/week to be split between (a) his pocket—spending money (b) 529 education plan—college savings plan and (c) Roth IRA and (d) his savings account. Total deduction annual: $20,800.

6) **MEDICAL EXPENSES:** Since the TaxSaver's income is so high, they have not been able to deduct medical expenses on their personal tax return. The rule is medical expenses must be more than 7.5% of their income. (If 7.5% of their income was $10,000 and they had $10,001 in medical expenses, they would get credit for $1.) So I recommended setting up a medical expense reimbursement plan (MERP) – which would allow them to write off all of their medical expenses, including health insurance premiums, prescriptions, co-pays, braces, exams, therapy, etc. Each time they have a medical expense, they simply submit their receipt to the company, which in turn reimburses the TaxSavers. Last year's medical expenses for the family of 6 was $12,529. This reimbursement is tax free money that they do not have to report on their tax return!

7) **RETIREMENT PLAN:** My tax planning service includes a visit with a Certified Financial Planner who assesses the family's financial goals and retirement needs, then structures a plan to meet those goals. The most favorable plan for the TaxSavers was a 401(K) plan which would allow each spouse to contribute $16,500 each year plus 25% of their income. Their retirement plan results in a deduction of $68,000.

8) **DAYCARE:** With one child in daycare, the TaxSavers paid almost $7000 in child care fees last year and received absolutely no credit on their tax return. A Dependant Care Reimbursement Account allows them a maximum deduction of

$5000 each year. The TaxSavers have the money deducted from their salary and every week after they pay daycare fees, submit the receipt and are reimbursed 100% on a tax-free basis from the money set aside in their account.

9) **ATHLETIC FACILITY:** Since the TaxSavers have a pool, trampoline, a basketball/tennis court and exercise equipment on the business premises (at home), and all employees (the family) have access to it, they can write off the repair, maintenance and purchase of equipment as an athletic facility. Last years' expenses were $2,820.

10) **EQUIPMENT/FURNITURE LEASING:** Mr.TaxSaver purchased all the equipment and furniture the business uses. The business can then rent the equipment and furniture on a monthly basis from Mr. TaxSaver. Based on local rental company rates, he is able to charge $1970 a month which results in a deduction of $23,640. He will need to claim this income on his personal tax return, but against it we will write off the depreciation, maintenance and repair of the equipment and furniture.

**THE RESULTS:**

|  |  |
|---|---|
| a. Home Office | $ 30,000 |
| b. Automobile | $ 18,250 |
| c. Salary for Owners | $140,000 |
| d. Salary for Children | $ 52,000 |
| e. Medical Expenses | $ 12,529 |
| f. Retirement Plan | $ 68,000 |
| g. Daycare | $ 5,000 |
| h. Athletic Facility | $ 2,820 |
| i. Equipment Leasing | $ 23,640 |

Total : $352,239

**TAXABLE INCOME IS REDUCED BY $352,239!**

After deducting the normal business expenses the TaxSavers have reduced their taxable income to $0!

*The TaxSavers now operate their business tax free!*

It is very important to have all your i's dotted and your t's crossed when it comes to substantiating documentation for the Internal Revenue Service. All of your paperwork must conform to IRS guidelines, be accurate and in place, in order for you to claim the deductions. You must also adopt any of the measures you choose to use through a meeting of your Board of Directors.

It is vitally important to keep receipts, mileage logs, and actually write checks from the company to yourself to substantiate expenses and create a paper trail. The best strategy is to hire a professional bookkeeper/accountant that understands your tax planning strategy to keep your books and paperwork in order.

For questions about tax planning, please feel free to contact me at: larisa@abundantreturns.com.

## About Larisa

### *I Paid More Taxes Than a Billionaire!!*

I started Abundant Returns Tax Service back in 1991 after seeing on TV that Ross Perot, then presidential candidate and CEO of a multi-billion dollar corporation, **paid less than $2000 in personal income taxes!**

I just couldn't believe it because…

I made $35,000 that year and paid *More Than $4000* in federal taxes alone!!!

I paid **more than double** the taxes a Billionaire paid!!!

I was flabbergasted to say the least.

"He's a billionaire," I kept saying to myself. "How is it legal for me to pay more taxes than a billionaire?"

I kept tossing it around in my head. I just couldn't believe it. I worried about how I was going to pay the rent. I struggled to buy a bus pass every week. I had to make "arrangements" every month to pay my utility bills. My grocery budget was $15/week and I was paying more income taxes than a billionaire?!!!

It made absolutely no sense to me. It still makes no sense to me…20 years later! (If I think about it long enough, I still get mad.)

This was an "a-ha" moment for me—a life lesson that shattered my very sheltered view of reality. I learned two very valuable lessons–- life is not fair and rich people can avoid income taxes.

So I got busy.

I took several income tax preparation courses.

I read hundreds of books on taxes. I've prepared thousands of tax returns.

I worked for the IRS and a local tax office. I learned about taxes and how to use the tax law to my advantage. I learned how to live "tax free" like billionaires do.

Now I'm ready to share that knowledge with you so you can "Keep More Money In Your Pocket" too. In my ebook, "Pay Yourself Instead of Uncle Sam", I explore many tax strategies that will help you reduce your taxes as low as possible. You can find it at http://small-business-tax-info.com.

For special offers to readers of this book and to join my mailing list, go to: http://small-business-tax-info.com/breakingthecode.
You can contact me at: larisa@abundantreturns.com or feel free to give me a call at: (770) 451-6330.

# CHAPTER 15

# Health Care Tax Changes

## By Richard A. Lindsey, CPA

In March 2010, two two pieces of legislation, the Patient Protection and Affordable Care Act and the Health Care and Education Reconciliation Act of 2010 were signed into law. Together these pieces of legislation make the most significant reform to health care in the United States since the enactment of Medicare under the Johnson administration in 1965.

You may think health care reform is something new, but attempts to reform health care are not limited to the Johnson, Clinton and Obama administrations. Look back a century and you'll see that President Theodore Roosevelt ran for the presidency on a platform supporting national health insurance. It was included in the original Social Security Act. President Richard Nixon and Ted Kennedy almost reached an agreement on health care reform, but were derailed by Nixon's early departure from office.

It may not be a new idea, but Obama and the Congress have placed a huge administrative burden on small businesses.

Health Care Reform may already have you confused, but it's not your fault. The massive health care reform bills were intentionally designed so that it was impossible for any one person to comprehend. We know those in Congress didn't even read it. They admitted it!

How can you be expected to understand it if no one has explained it to you? So, take a deep breath and relax, we're about to take aim at this confusion and make (at least some) things as clear as possible. In this chapter, we're going to focus on the tax changes that affect small businesses.

Starting in 2010, government subsidies became available for small businesses to provide employees health insurance coverage. However, the law does not require any business to purchase insurance for its employees. That said, incentives for small businesses to provide their employees with group health insurance coverage are noteworthy.

Businesses with 10 or fewer full-time-equivalent employees (FTEs) earning less than $25,000 a year, on average, are eligible for a tax credit of 35% of qualifying employee health insurance premium costs. Companies with between 11 and 25 workers and an average wage up to $50,000 are eligible for partial credits. Beginning in 2014, the small business tax credits will cover 50% of premiums through 2016.

Except in the case of a tax-exempt employer, the credit applies only to income taxes. Normally an unused general business credit can be carried back (by a small business) 5 years and forward 20 years. However, an unused credit amount cannot be carried back to a year before the effective date of the credit, so any unused credit amount for 2010 can only be carried forward.

The number of FTEs is determined by including not only the hours employees are paid for working, but also paid vacation, illness, holiday, or other paid-leave time. The employer may calculate the total number of hours of service for determining the number of FTEs by either determining the actual number of hours for which payment has been made, or by using days-worked or weeks-worked equivalents, claiming credit for eight hours for any day or 40 hours for any week in which an employee would be credited for at least one hour of work.

In calculating the credit, the employer can only include premiums which the employer paid and incurred an expense. Amounts withheld from employees are not counted, including those withheld under a Sec. 125 cafeteria plan.

> **Example.** *If Wonder Wags pays 80% of the premiums for employee's coverage (with employees paying the other 20%), only the 80% premium amount paid by Wonder Wags counts in calculating the credit.*

In addition, the amount of an employer's premium payments that counts when calculating the credit, may not exceed the average premium for the small group market in the particular state (or an area within a state) in which the employer offers coverage for the same arrangement. The average premium for the small group market in a state (or area) will be determined by the Department of Health and Human Services (HHS). The IRS has published this information online at www.irs.gov.

The number of an employer's FTEs is determined by dividing (a) the total hours for which the employer pays wages to employees during the year (but not more than 2,080 hours for any employee), by (b) 2,080. The result, if not a whole number, is then rounded down to the next lowest whole number.

> **Example.** *For the 2010 tax year, Cycle Hut pays 5 employees for 2,080 hours of service each, 3 employees for 1,040 hours of service each, and 1 employee for 2,300 hours of service.*
>
> *The number of Cycle Hut's FTEs would be calculated as follows:*
>
> *1. Total hours not exceeding 2,080 per employee is the sum of*

*10,400 hours for the 5 employees paid for 2,080 hours each (5 x 2,080)*

*+ 3,120 hours for the 3 employees paid for 1,040 hours each (3 x 1,040)*

*+ 2,080 hours for the 1 employee paid for 2,300 hours (maximum of 2,080)*

---

*15,600 TOTAL hours*

*2. So, the FTEs = 7 (15,600 divided by 2,080 = 7.5, rounded down to the next lowest whole number)*

The tax credit is phased out as firm size and average wage increases.

Presuming the number of an employer's FTEs exceeds 10, or if the average annual wages exceed $25,000, the amount of the credit is proportionally reduced. If the number of FTEs exceeds 10, the reduction would be calculated by multiplying the otherwise applicable credit amount by a fraction, the numerator of which is the number of FTEs in excess of 10 and the denominator of which is 15. Full phase-out occurs with 25 FTEs.

Leased employees are included in the count.

The amount of average annual wages is determined by first dividing (a) the total wages paid by the employer to employees during the employer's tax year, by (b) the number of the employer's FTEs for the year. The result is then rounded down to the nearest $1,000. For this purpose, wages means wages as defined for FICA purposes (without regard to the wage base limitation).

> **Example.** *In the 2010 tax year, Candy's Cakes pays $224,000 in wages and has 10 FTEs.*
>
> *Candy's Cakes average annual wages would be $22,000 ($224,000 divided by 10 = $22,400, rounded down to the nearest $1,000).*

Assuming an employer's average annual wages exceed $25,000, the reduction is determined by multiplying the otherwise applicable credit amount by a fraction, the numerator of which is the amount by which the average annual wages exceed $25,000 and the denominator of which is $25,000. Full phase-out occurs when average annual wages reach $50,000.

For an employer with both more than 10 FTEs and average annual wages exceeding $25,000, the reduction is the sum of the amount of the two reductions. This sum may reduce the credit to zero for some employers with fewer than 25 FTEs and an average annual wage less than $50,000.

> **Example.** For the 2010 tax year, presume that Cleaning Diva, a qualified employer, has 12 FTEs earning average annual wages of $30,000. Cleaning Diva pays $96,000 in health care premiums for those employees (which does not exceed the average premium for the small group market in the employer's state).
>
> The credit is calculated as follows:
>
> 1. Initial amount of credit determined before any reduction: (35% x $96,000) = $33,600
>
> 2. Credit reduction for FTEs in excess of 10: ($33,600 x 2/15) = $4,480
>
> 3. Credit reduction for average annual wages in excess of $25,000: ($33,600 x $5,000/$25,000) = $6,720
>
> 4. Total credit reduction: ($4,480 + $6,720) = $11,200
>
> **5. Total 2010 tax credit: ($33,600 – $11,200) = $22,400**

In calculating the employer's deduction for health insurance premiums, the amount of premiums that can be deducted is reduced by the amount of the credit.

The credit is available for regular health insurance premiums and add-on dental and vision coverage. Employers can still qualify for the credit if they receive state health care tax credits.

Seasonal workers are disregarded in determining FTEs and average annual wages unless the seasonal worker works for the employer on more than 120 days during the taxable year, although premiums paid on their behalf may be counted in determining the amount of the credit.

A sole proprietor, a partner in a partnership, a shareholder owning more than two percent of an S corporation, and any owner of more than five percent of other businesses are not considered employees for the purposes of the credit. Therefore, the wages or hours of these business owners and partners are not counted in determining either the number of FTEs or the amount of the average annual wages, and the premiums paid on their behalf are not counted in determining the amount of the credit.

Further, under the family attribution rules, a family member of any of the business owners or partners is also not considered an employee for purposes of the credit. For this purpose, a family member is defined as a child (or descendant of a child); a sibling or step-sibling; a parent (or an cestor of a parent); a step-parent; a niece or nephew; an aunt or uncle; or a son-in-law, daughter-in-law, father-in-law, mother-in-law, brother-in-law or sister-in-law. Note who's missing from the list: *a spouse.*

For 2012, businesses will be required to include the value of health care benefits they provide to employees on W-2s, beginning with W-2s for 2011. The W-2s going out in 2012 will reflect coverage provided in 2011.

While it is expected that most 2011 W-2s will be issued in January 2012, Form W-2s reflecting the new health insurance information must be available no later than February 1, 2011, in the event a terminating employee requests one. This is because employees are entitled to request their Form W-2s early if they terminate employment during the year.

Plans for which coverage costs must be reported include medical, prescription, executive physicals, Medicare supplemental policies, and employee assistance programs. Coverages under dental and vision plans must also be included unless they are "standalone" plans.

Continuing health-care insurance under COBRA must also be considered in reporting the value of employee's health care costs on their W-2 forms for 2011.

However, the cost of coverage under health flexible spending accounts, health savings accounts, and specific disease or hospital/ fixed indemnity plans is excluded from the reporting.

Hidden deep inside the massive 2,409 page health care reform bill are a few lines which will unleash a flurry of paperwork on unsuspecting businesses. The new law makes key changes in 1099 requirements. First, it expands the scope from only services to include all tangible goods and second, it requires that 1099s be issued not just to individuals but also to corporations.

Beginning in 2012 companies will have to issue 1099 forms not just to contract workers but to any individual or corporation from which they buy more than $600 in goods or services in a tax year.

Businesses will have to issue billions of new tax documents each year.

Under the new rules if you buy a new computer from Best Buy, you'll have to send them a 1099. A laundromat that buys soap each week from a local distributor will have to send the supplier a 1099 at year end. The local restauranteur will have to send 1099s to each of his food suppliers, linen or laundry service, beer and liquor distributors, electrical utility, and on and on.

Payments to tax-exempt organizations should continue to be exempt from information reporting under the new law. Debit or credit card payments will also be exempt from the reporting requirements since these transactions will already be covered by reporting requirements on payment card processors.

"It's a pretty heavy administrative burden," particularly for small businesses without an in-house accounting staff according to the National Federation of Independent Businesses.

The IRS estimates that more than $300 billion is lost in unreported tax revenue each year. Using 1099s to document millions of transactions that now go untracked is one way they believe they can close the tax gap.

While the notion of mailing a tax form to Office Depot or Sam's Club each year likely seems absurd to most small business owners, it gets worse. The biggest headache will be gathering and inputting the names, addresses and taxpayer ID numbers for every vendor you do business with.

Increased record keeping could weigh heavily on small businesses. At a minimum, a significant amount of time and training is going to be required to gather, sort and input the data needed for every vendor. Even the smallest of businesses will require software to help them maintain good records.

Ignoring the requirements could lead to disaster. Businesses which fail to file information returns or file incomplete returns could be subject to a $50 penalty for each required return. For an intentional disregard of the requirement, the penalty could increase to $100 per return or more.

It might be helpful to think of the new reporting requirements as similar to payroll. In a sense, America is going on a payroll style reporting system beginning in 2012

High-income taxpayers will be hit with two big tax hikes: a tax increase on wages and a new tax on investments.

The new law imposes an additional 0.9% Medicare tax on wages above $200,000 for individuals and $250,000 for married couples filing jointly. In addition, for higher-income households, the new law adds a 3.8% tax on net investment income.

Currently, all wages are subject to a 2.9% Medicare tax. Workers and employers pay 1.45% each. Self-employed people pay both halves of the tax (but are allowed to deduct half of this amount for income tax purposes).

Under the provisions of the new law, which take effect in 2013, most taxpayers will continue to pay the 1.45% Medicare tax, but single people earning more than $200,000 and married couples earning more than $250,000 will be taxed an additional 0.9% (2.35% in total) on the excess over those base amounts. Self-employed persons will pay 3.8% on earnings over those thresholds.

It should be noted that the $200,000/$250,000 thresholds aren't indexed for inflation, so it is likely that more and more people will be subject to the higher tax in coming years.

Beginning in 2013, a Medicare tax will, for the first time, be applied to investment income. A new 3.8% tax will be imposed on net investment income of single taxpayers with adjusted gross income above $200,000 and joint filers over $250,000 (unindexed).

Net investment income is interest, dividends, royalties, rents, gross income from a trade or business involving passive activities, and net gain from disposition of property (other than property held in a trade or business). Net investment income is reduced by the deductions that are allocable to that income. However, the new tax won't apply to income in tax-deferred retirement accounts such as 401(k) plans.

## About Richard

Richard A. Lindsey, CPA, also known as the "Renegade CPA," is a small business tax expert, consultant, speaker and author who helps companies and their owners keep the money they've earned instead of handing it over to Uncle Sam. He has 19 years experience as a CPA and 15 years of "in-the-trenches" work before that in the family business.

While working in the family business, Richard returned to the University of South Alabama in 1989 to earn his Master of Accounting (MAcc) degree. Upon graduation, he joined the University as an adjunct professor of accounting and a local accounting firm as a staff accountant. Richard became a partner in Zevac & Lindsey in 2000.

With Richard you get someone who understands the concerns of small business owners, someone who is focused on taxes and how they affect your business, and someone who will explain what you need to know and what you need to do about it in plain English.

To learn more about Richard, the Renegade CPA, and how you can receive free special reports and invaluable tax tips without having to wade through all the boring rhetoric and tax mumbo-jumbo, visit: www.TaxSaverTips.com or send an email to: ZevacLindsey@comcast.net.

# CHAPTER 16

# The Audit And Beyond: Taking On The IRS

By Salvatore P. Candela EA, ABA, ATA, RFC
The TaxAdvocate Group

*"America is a land of taxation that was
founded to avoid taxation."*
~ Laurence J. Peter

When you do something on your tax return that's obviously not kosher and an IRS audit flags it, there's not a whole lot you can do about it. Taking a deduction that's not allowed, hiding income that plainly *is* income or doing anything else that's blatantly against IRS rules means you have to pay the price if you're caught. Lying about it can only get you into more trouble (just so you know – people go to jail in this country for lying to federal agents, which is what an IRS revenue agent is, not for failing to pay their taxes).

But what happens when the IRS fights you about a tax issue that you believe is *right*? Or that, at least, is a gray issue?

That's usually when someone comes to me. I'm an Enrolled Agent. If you don't know what that is, you're no different than most Americans. If you're ever in a position where you have a tax problem with the IRS, however, you should know what an EA is. An EA can be your best friend – and your best weapon in fighting your cause.

In this chapter, I'll give you a broad overview of what your options are when the IRS does come after you for money you don't believe you owe – and what the best strategies are that will enable you to walk away with either a radically reduced tax bill – or, best of all, no tax bill at all.

The main reason I became an EA? Well, what started it all was the fact that I hated my father's accountant. I'll explain that a little later, but first, you should understand what an EA is.

## THE ROLE OF AN ENROLLED AGENT

An Enrolled Agent is someone legally authorized and recognized by the IRS to represent a taxpayer at an audit or an audit appeal. Because they have a federal license instead of a state license, unlike a CPA or a lawyer, they can represent anyone anywhere in the country in an IRS dispute.

Also unlike a CPA or a lawyer, an EA only earns that designation because of his or her extensive knowledge of the federal tax code. There are only two ways to become an EA – either you work for the IRS for at least five years in a capacity in which you have to interpret the tax code on a regular basis, or you must take a very demanding two-day exam.

How demanding is it? Well, first of all, less than a third of those who take the exam pass it. Second of all - you're not allowed to use a calculator! Have you ever tried to calculate depreciation without a calculator? Don't. You'll hurt yourself.

Why would you want an EA instead of the person who prepared your tax return to represent you at an audit? Well, if that person is not a CPA or an attorney, they *are not allowed* to represent you to the IRS. They can go along to the audit and explain what they did on your tax return – but they are not allowed to argue on your behalf.

And, to be frank, you may not *want* them to argue on your behalf, even if they are a CPA. CPAs, contrary to most people's beliefs, are generally not tax experts – they are accounting experts, licensed by whatever state they practice in to help with accounting problems. When they studied to become CPAs, they primarily learned GAAP – Generally Accepted Accounting Practices – and took a little tax coursework. They don't necessarily know all the nuances of the IRS regulations.

Enrolled Agents, however, are certified by the Department of Treasury as experts on tax code. The IRS doesn't care about GAAP when they pursue an audit – they want to know how the tax laws back up what's on a return. It's more of a legal battle than a numbers game – that's why being an EA is as close to practicing law as someone without a law license can do as a profession.

And it's also why an EA can do you the most good when you do have an IRS dispute you need to resolve. An EA can go toe-to-toe with the government on the most complex tax issues, because an EA knows as much as *they* do – or possibly even more in some cases.

## THE MAKING OF AN EA

So how did I come to be an EA? I said earlier it was because I hated my father's accountant – which is only partially true. My father's accountant was actually the motivating force that caused me to begin my tax education.

Like many young people just going out into the workforce, when it came time to get my taxes done, I went to the person my father used. In that accountant's eyes, I was a 'pain in the neck'. I asked a lot of questions, questions he said he didn't have time to answer.

So I decided I was going to find out those answers for myself.

I began taking accounting classes on my own, just so I'd be able to do my own taxes. And it fascinated me. Maybe I'm weird, but I started educating myself more and more on the tax code, reading books and taking more classes.

Then I started to put all that education to work outside of my own returns – I began doing returns for friends and family members at no charge, just because, believe it or not, it was a pleasurable hobby. I found it a satisfying challenge to do these returns and test my knowledge. And when I didn't know something, I made sure to find out more about it. I took more and more classes, did more and more returns, until finally I felt ready to open a little office with a barebones staff to do returns professionally.

As I continued on my way with my new tax business, I began to hear more and more about "EA's" – and started to research just what those two letters were all about. I found out that an En-rolled Agent was an IRS-certified taxpayer representative who had to be an expert on tax code. That was right in my wheel-house. I took the summer off and studied for that backbreaking exam I discussed earlier in this chapter – and I passed my first time around.

Terrific, I was an official EA. But, much like a lawyer who grad-uates from law school, I may have known everything about the tax code, but I had no idea how to actually do anything for a taxpayer. I didn't know how to prepare a protest, put together an Offer in Compromise or deal with anything more advanced than routine IRS paperwork.

That meant three more years of education through the National Tax Practice Institute (NTPI), and finally, in the year 2000, I be-came an NTPI Fellow, which meant I was prepared to offer my clients' the finest representation skills available before the IRS.

Since then our business, The TaxAdvocate Group, has continued to grow and we now have three offices, two in New York (in Queens and Manhattan) and one in Fort Lauderdale, Florida. I usually have anywhere from 20 to 30 active audit cases at a time that I work on.

I'm proud to say that I aggressively represent my clients if I think they have a legitimate case against the IRS. I don't back down and I will argue up and down (and sometimes sideways if necessary!) to fight for my clients' interests.

## THE AUDIT

The first sign of trouble with the IRS is when you're notified of being audited. If you ever get an audit letter, the number one thing I would advise you (whether you hire me or not) is *don't ever represent yourself* with the IRS.

Why? Because the IRS agent serving as the auditor represents the government, not you. He or she does not have your interests at heart. You need someone to advocate your position – and it shouldn't be you. It should be someone who understands the tax code and can argue knowledgably on your behalf.

As a matter of fact, I even advise the taxpayer not to go to his or her own audit. You will get too personally involved and that could come back to haunt you.

For example, when IRS agents ask me a question about my client's return, I give as short an answer as possible. They like to just stare at me to see if I'll say anything more – to be more accurate, to see if I'll say too much and reveal something I shouldn't. Silence is one of their chief weapons – because a taxpayer, not knowing how they work, will continue talking until they either end up contradicting themselves or say something that the IRS agent will pounce on.

An expert representative, however, will only say enough to answer the question. We know when to keep our mouths shut.

The other thing is that you never know what kind of mind set the auditor will have. Some come in 100% against the taxpayer's position, no matter what. These people you don't even bother arguing with – better to wait and appeal the audit (which, to be honest, is what you really ultimately want anyway) instead. Some will be tough but fair. But the main thing to remember is that the auditor is there to push the government agenda. He or she is not there to 'make nice' with you or bend over backwards to accommodate a questionable deduction. They are there because a mistake has been flagged and they want you to pay for that mistake

And that's why an audit is the *worst* place to attempt to negotiate a settlement.

If you think you're right but the auditor will not budge, then you have the right to speak to the group manager of the auditor's team. Most of the time, however, the group manager won't do anything to overrule the auditor's initial decision – but it's still important to speak to the group manager, however, in order to establish your first step to disagreeing with the audit outcome.

## THE AUDIT APPEAL

You might think that filing an audit appeal is a useless step. You're still arguing with the IRS, which is the agency that made the initial decision against you in the audit, right?

Yes, that's true. But the audit appeal process is designed to *encourage* a settlement if the taxpayer has a legitimate case.

Let's take a few steps back and explain how the appeal process works. You'll receive the Reviewing Agent's Report (the RAR) after your audit is over. With that report comes the IRS form that you can fill out to file an appeal to your audit. If the amount in question is less than $25,000 for a tax year, you can do an informal appeal (the overall total can be more than that – for instance, the IRS may say you owe $40,000, but if $17,000 is from one tax year and $23,000 is from another, you can still do an informal appeal). If it's more than $25,000 for a single tax year, you can file a formal appeal.

In either case, you have 30 days to file that appeal – which is exactly what you *should* do. Because, again, you have a much better chance at a beneficial settlement if you move forward to an appeal.

That's because appeal officers are 'a completely different animal' to the auditors. Their goal is to work out differences. Again, if something is just plain 'black and white' wrong, you won't get any further with an audit appeal. But if it is something that's open to interpretation – and with 80,000 pages in the tax code, there is a LOT open to interpretation – the appeals process could very well work in your favor.

Why? Basically the IRS doesn't want a case to drag on too long. More importantly, it doesn't want most cases to go to the next step – tax court.

Auditors aren't allowed to consider the implications of a taxpayer case advancing to tax court – the appeal officer must. They have to think about the consequences of the government losing a case in tax court – and possibly upending part of the tax code as it applies to *all* taxpayers, which could ultimately cost the IRS a lot of money. So they research an appeal and look at the law and figure out what their chances of winning in tax court might be.

That means if they think they could lose, your appeal will probably "win."

## TAX COURT

Let's say your appeal outcome isn't to your satisfaction. The IRS then gives you 90 days to file a case with the United States Tax Court. The Tax Court was established by the U.S. Constitution and has 19 presidentially-appointed members.

An EA is not allowed to represent you to the Tax Court unless they pass an even more rigorous exam – an exam that has a passing rate of only 3 or 4%. This is one river I can't take the time to cross, as I would probably have to take a year off to study for it. One colleague of mine failed this exam the first time – and the second time, when they sent him his results, he was so nervous it took him two days before he could bring himself to open the envelope!

You can only present your case to the Tax Court once (although in some cases you can appeal). But, much like the audit appeals process, the mindset here is to work things out. That's why 98% of all cases never go to trial at the Tax Court – the government wants to settle these cases and make them go away.

In conclusion, I'd like to talk about one of my most interesting cases to demonstrate how a simple case where all the facts are in a taxpayer's favor can still make an audit appeal necessary.

My client was one of the original investors in *Vitaminwater*; he put in $30,000 to help launch the brand. In 2007, the Coca-Cola Company bought out the company and my client's share of the sale was 3.5 million dollars. So far, so good. Okay, more than good – incredibly amazing.

Coke agreed to pay my client 90% of the amount in 2007 – and the remaining 10% over 2008 and 2009. The problem was that the 1099 Coke sent to my client in 2007 had the entire amount on it. In other words, in the IRS' eyes, my client received $350,000 in 2007 that, in reality, he never did. The IRS kept insisting he owed taxes on the money anyway.

We ended up filing a 44 page audit appeal that ultimately saved my client $116,000 in taxes for 2007 – but it wouldn't have happened unless we *did* file that appeal.

When you're right, it's worth the fight. Again, the audit is not where you can usually win that fight – the appeal is. When you have the right representative going to the mat for you, you can take on the IRS and prevail.

I do it every day.

## About Salvatore

Salvatore P. Candela, EA has been preparing taxes since 1986, passed the EA exam in 1997, became an Enrolled Agent in 1998, and a Fellow of NTPI (National Tax Practice Institute) in 2000, and has been a featured speaker around the country.

He has earned the following credentials from the Accreditation Council for Accountancy and Taxation – Accredited Business Accountant (ABA), and Accredited Tax Advisor (ATA). He has also earned the credential of Registered Financial Consultant (RFC) from the International Association of Registered Financial Consultants.

He is the owner and founder of The TaxAdvocate Group which is focused on tax controversy resolution – with offices in New York (Queens & Wall Street), Florida, and Michigan. His firm aggressively represents taxpayers before all administrative levels of the IRS, and is committed to helping taxpayers resolve their IRS problems – ***ONCE AND FOR ALL!***

Salvatore is a member of the National Association of Enrolled Agents (NAEA), the New York State Society of Enrolled Agents (NYSSEA), the National Society of Accountants (NSA), and the National Association of Tax Professionals (NATP). These memberships help him stay current with the constantly changing tax laws and enable him to protect taxpayer's rights.

# CHAPTER 17

# Tax Shelters

## By James (Jim) Henderson, CPA

**W**ebster defines a Tax Shelter as "a strategy, investment or tax code provision that reduces tax liability." Tax shelter investments were extremely popular when the maximum federal tax rate was 70% and above. Wealthy individuals were looking for ways to dramatically reduce their tax burden. Currently, the maximum federal rate stands at about half of the 70% figure. Combine this with the passage of the 1986 Tax Reform Act which dramatically limited tax losses from passive activities, and the tax shelter went the way of the Dodo Bird and the Sony Walkman.

There still exists, however, strategies and tax code provisions which can save any taxpayer significant tax dollars. These Tax Shelters are not just available for the wealthy, as almost anyone with a little proper advanced planning can avail themselves of their benefits.

I have been asked, "How can I save $100,000 in taxes?" Now it's pretty rare where one can save that amount in one transaction. However, much like the answer to the question "How do you eat an elephant?" ...the response "One bite at a time!" applies. Given the multitude of Tax Shelters available and being utilized over one's lifetime, tax savings of $100,000 and even more can easily be attained.

# People don't plan for failure, they just fail to plan!

One would think the logical next step would be to start researching all Tax Shelters. That would be like checking out all the homes available for sale around the world when you know you want a three-bedroom, two-bathroom condominium in Boston served by public transportation in the $400,000 range. The real first step to finding what Tax Shelters would be best for you is to know your Financial Plan.

What is your Financial Plan? In its most basic terms, it is the profile of where you are at versus where you want to be. It consists of both your cash inflows and outflows, as well as what you own and what you owe. Therefore, in order to get from your present profile point to a future profile point, you need a Financial Plan that is specifically tailored to your circumstances.

The first step to determine your current profile would be to gather your financial records, such as check registers, bank statements, brokerage statements, retirement accounts, property listings, insurance policies, credit card records, mortgage and other loan statements, etc. From these you can clearly determine where your inflows come from and where the outflows go. You can get a snapshot of what you own vs. what you owe. Hopefully you own more than you owe.

With this information, you can project where you want to be at some future point, then implement plans of action to get there. Examples would be: Pay off mortgage in 15 years, … have $500k in retirement by age 65, …buy a vacation home by age 45, … save $125k for college for each child.

## The Tax Man Cometh…

Financial Plans involve financial transactions, and it is a fact of life that in almost every financial transaction, taxes rear their ugly head. In fact, taxes can amount to 50% or more of a transaction's cost. If you reduce or eliminate the taxes, you keep more money in your pocket. Therefore, for each of your financial transactions, you have to identify the Tax Shelter (i.e., the strategy or tax code) which will save you tax dollars.

Now, how do you determine what you will save? You must know your marginal tax bracket. First, your marginal bracket is not the same as your average tax rate. Indeed, someone's average federal and state income tax rate could be 18% of total income, but their marginal rate is always higher, say 33%. Your marginal tax rate is how much your taxes will change for every marginal increase or decrease in income. So, even if you have an average tax rate of 18%, but a marginal rate of 33%, you know that an additional $3,000 of interest income will not cost you $540 in taxes, but close to $1,000.

Secondly, your marginal tax rate is not always just comprised of your federal and state income taxes. Other taxes could come into play. These include, among others, Social Security and Medicare taxes on wages (7.65% up to certain limits), self-employment taxes on unincorporated business earned income (15.3%) up to certain limits, penalties on premature retirement plan distributions (10% or more, depending on plan type), the Alternative Minimum Tax, and lower taxes on long-term capital gains and qualified dividends (currently maxed at 15%).

Thirdly, your marginal tax rate is always subject to change, depending on the year, the tax laws currently in effect, and your income level and type.

Lastly, you should look at the marginal tax rate not only for yourself, but for all members of your immediate family. A child's marginal tax rate, even after factoring in the provisions of the Kiddie Tax, can be much lower than that of a parent. Thus, shifting income to a child could save significant taxes for the family unit.

To keep it simple, we'll just deal with the following marginal tax rate assumptions:

| | **Combined**<br>(Rounded) |
|---|---|
| Federal income tax 28% and | |
| State income tax 5% | 33% |
| Social Security/Medicare 7.65% | 40% |
| Self-Employment 15.3% | 48% |

Since most taxpayers can count earned wages as a major in flow, let's look at Tax Shelters that may be available to them.

## Retire in Style

A large number of employers offer retirement plans, some even with company-match provisions. If your employer does not offer one, you can open up an IRA (Individual Retirement Account) on your own. As part of your Financial Plan, you want to retire some day and have enough money to live on, so a retirement account would fit the bill.

Let's say you want to save $100/week towards retirement. Doing this on your own, you would have to earn about $150/week to net $100/week after taxes assuming a 33% marginal tax rate. To add insult to injury, you would be taxed on the annual earnings on the investment account. Not a very good deal.

On the other hand, let's say your employer has a 401(k) retirement plan with an annual match of up to $1,000. If you placed $150/week into the plan, your net paycheck would remain the same as outlined above as if you would have saved $100/week after taxes. However, at the end of the year, you would have $8,800 in your 401(k) plan (52 x $150 + $1,000) vs. $5,200 in the investment account ($52 x $100), a $3,600 or over 67% increased annual savings benefit.

Contributions and earnings thereon within the retirement plan will grow tax-deferred until withdrawn. The normal assumption is that you will have a lower marginal tax rate when retired than during your working years. If you feel that your marginal tax rate may be the same or even higher when you are retired, then you may want to consider a Roth IRA. While you get no current deduction, contributions and earnings thereon will be tax-free if withdrawn during retirement.

The main reasons I like employer-sponsored plans are:

1. Funding is done at the payroll source, so funds are never available to you. I've always found that an individual's spending expands or contracts depending on the funds available. Therefore, the best laid plans of saving on your own can, and usually do, go awry.

2. You retain control of all your funds, rather than having a portion gone to the government via taxes.

3. With control come options. While funds should be used for retirement, in emergency or financial crisis situations, the funds are available through loan or withdrawal. While taxes and penalties could ensue, better to have the fund availability option than nothing at all.

## Load Up at the Cafeteria

Another Tax Shelter benefit for wage-earners would be employer-sponsored cafeteria plans. Under such pans, employees can select from a smorgasbord of benefits, most on a pre-tax basis. Choices would include health and dental insurance, medical and dependent care assistance plans (DCAP).

There is a lot of misinformation out there about these plans, so much so that people are not participating when they really should. I've heard things like "I can deduct medical anyway, why do I need to join the plan?" or "I can get the child care credit, so why do I need the DCAP?" or "my wife's hairdresser said it was a bad idea."

While there may be a small portion of truth in the above (except for the hairdresser's opinion), the full truth is that you will usually save much more in taxes by participating than not. Take medical expenses for example. While it is true that medical costs are indeed deductible, they are only allowable as itemized deductions and only if all medical costs presently exceed 7.5% of adjusted gross income which, in my experience, is very rare.

So, if you participated and had $5,000 in health insurance and out-of-pocket medical, you would save 40% (federal, state, Social Security and Medicare) in taxes, or $2,000. In the vast majority of cases, little or no tax savings would result if you tried to deduct medical as an itemized deduction.

By contributing $5,000 to a DCAP to be used towards Junior's pre-school tuition to allow you and your spouse to work would save the family unit the same 40% in taxes or $2,000. Claiming the child care credit for one child on your tax return usually results in only a $600 tax savings, or $1,400 less.

## Using "Your" Shelter as a Tax Shelter

The number one tax shelter for most taxpayers results from home ownership. The federal tax code and some states will allow deductions for home mortgage interest and real estate taxes. Absent these deductions, taxpayers who rent their homes normally take the standard deduction in computing their taxes.

Taxpayers are allowed to take the higher of the standard deduction or their itemized deductions. Itemized deductions include: Medical, Taxes, Interest, Contributions, Casualty & Theft Losses, Job Related Costs and Miscellaneous. For further details as to what are included as itemized deductions, please refer to the IRS web site at www.irs.gov

This site contains a wealth of information for this and other tax inquiries you may have.

To demonstrate the tax savings a single or married taxpayer could attain through home ownership is outlined below based on the following assumptions (obviously results will vary, based on your particular circumstances and tax year):

Single individual, earning $55,000, buying a condominium for $150,000 and financing $120,000.

Married individuals, combined earnings of $100,000, buying a home for $275,000 and financing $220,000.

|  | Single | Married |
|---|---|---|
| Mortgage interest | $6,600 | $12,050 |
| Real Estate taxes | 2,700 | 4,300 |
| State income tax | 2,500 | 4,500 |
| Contributions and other | 1,200 | 2,100 |
| Total itemized | 13,000 | 22,950 |
| Standard deduction | 5,800 | 9,750 |
| Excess deductions | 7,200 | 13,200 |
| Marginal Tax Rate Bracket | 33% | 33% |
| Tax Savings Per Year | 2,400 | 4,400 |
| Tax Savings Per Month | $200 | $367 |

Not only do you get tax benefits while owning a home, but a husband and wife can get up to a $500k gain exclusion when they sell their home in the future. This gain exclusion provision could save you about $100k in taxes!

## Home is where the office is

If you are required to maintain a home office as a condition of employment, or you are self-employed and work out of your home as your principle place of business, you may be allowed a home office deduction. You may think that it may not make much of a difference as the major home deductions of mortgage interest and real estate taxes are already allowed as itemized deductions. While this is true, all the other home ownership costs (including repairs, maintenance, insurance, utilities, depreciation, condo fees, etc.) would now move into the deduction calculation column. Additionally, the portion of your mortgage interest and real estate taxes related to the home office could save you an additional 15.3% in taxes if you are self-employed.

Let's say that you have a qualifying home office and $10,000 of previously non-deductible home ownership costs. If you use 15% of your home for business, then roughly $1,500 of additional deductions would be allowed on your return. This could save you roughly $500 as an employee, or roughly $720 as a self-employed individual.

## It's a Family Affair

It has been shown that raising a child to age 18 could cost upwards of $250k, and paying for four years of college could set you back another $250k. So, for the potential $500k investment, you should be able to get some tax benefits in return. The tax code is friendly where dependent children are involved. The myriad of benefits include dependency deduction, child tax credit, child care credit, adoption credit, education tax credits and deductions, college 529 savings plans, earned income credit, etc. While these may seem like a lot, and I am not minimizing their benefits, the simple fact is that you will not come anywhere close to recouping your $500k.

An often overlooked planning tool is utilizing dependents lower tax brackets. This works with earned income (i.e., wages), but does not fully work for unearned income because of the applicability of the Kiddie Tax for dependent children. Still, under present law, the first $950 of unearned income could be tax free, and the next $950 could then be taxed at the dependent's lower tax rate.

Therefore, a gifting program to move assets to the next generation could save the family some significant tax dollars. However, this strategy could backfire if you think you will be eligible for college financial aid. Assets in a child's name are assessed at a higher percentage in the financial aid formula than assets in a parent's name. This generally would reduce your aid eligibility.

## Practice Nepotism

If you have your own small closely-held business, like I do, then you almost always have your children help out with various business tasks. Whether it's stamping and sealing envelopes and cleaning the office at a young age, to doing more complex tasks as they mature, children can be a valuable asset to any thriving business. Some of you may now be saying "and the best part, ...they are free!" I want you to rethink that because you may be giving away tax dollars needlessly.

Let's say you are self-employed. You have 2 children and set aside $50 a week for each of them for allowance, spending money or savings. In order to have, after taxes, $100 available weekly, or $5,200 per year, you would have to earn $10,000 per year. Indeed you would lose $4,800 to taxes at a 48% rate (Federal, State and Self-Employment).

Instead, what if you put each of your children on the payroll for $5,000 each per year? These wages would reduce your annual taxable income by $10,000, thus saving you the aforementioned $4,800 in taxes. Now you may be saying, "what about payroll taxes the business would have to pay on the wages, and the income taxes your children would have to pay on their earnings?"

If your children are less than 18 years old and work for their parents in an unincorporated business, then they are not subject to social security and medicare taxes, for either the employee or employer portions. Additionally they are not subject to federal unemployment and most state unemployment and other assessments.

Well what about income taxes for the children? As their wages are earned income and not subject to the Kiddie Tax, they can each utilize their standard deduction, currently $5,800, to reduce taxable income to zero. So as long as their total income is less than the standard deduction, they pay no federal income tax, and in most cases, would not be subject to state income tax.

## ROTH IRA vs. COLLEGE 529 SAVINGS Plans

Some may think that it would be best to take some or all of the money earned by the children in the above example and place it in a College 529 Savings Plan. While I truly like these plans, they may not be the best investment in this particular circumstance, and could actually cause some unintended negative consequences. A better choice could be a Roth IRA in the child's name. Here's why.

529 Plans are similar to Roths in that they both offer tax deferred growth and tax free treatment if funds are used for their stated purposes. So if you use the 529 plan funds for qualified education expenses, the earnings are tax free. Roth distributions in retirement are likewise tax free.

What if 529 funds are not used for their stated purpose? Let's say Junior gets a full scholarship, or Junior is not the college type and starts his own business after high school, or Junior works, stays home and takes night classes at the inexpensive community college? If the 529 funds are taken out for non-educational purposes, then not only would the account earnings be taxable, but also would be subject to a 10% penalty tax. Not a good result.

Also, if you qualify for financial aid, savings in 529 plans actually count against you and reduce your financial aid award. Additionally, any funds from a 529 plan used for educational costs render those same costs ineligible for any education credit or deduction tax benefit.

Instead, let's say that you put up to $5,000 (the Roth annual limit) into each child's Roth account. Later, the account principle can be withdrawn for college costs without any tax consequence. If the earnings are then withdrawn for college, they will be taxed, however they will not be subject to the 10% Roth penalty tax on early distributions as paying for college costs is one of the penalty exceptions.

As retirement funds are usually not an assessable asset for financial aid purposes, funding a Roth IRA should not hurt you from a financial aid standpoint. Using Roth funds should not affect your eligibility for any education credit or deduction tax benefit. Lastly, if the Roth funds are not needed for college, then they can be retained and used for other purposes, such as buying a home, later higher education costs, retirement, etc., with little or no tax or penalty cost if proper planning is employed. Principal withdrawals will generally always be tax-free.

## Gimme Shelter!

So in conclusion, if you have a Financial Plan and truly understand the tax implications of each financial transaction that are part of your plan, then you will go a long way to minimizing the potentially largest financial transaction cost, namely taxes. Every tax dollar saved stays in your pocket to be used as you desire. *Remember, tax evasion is a crime, tax avoidance is just plain smart.*

The tax strategies above are presented to demonstrate the potential savings which can be attained. As everyone's circumstance is different, I would strongly recommend that you consult a qualified professional who can help you with your plan. Trying to do it on your own would be just plain dumb, and the consequences dire.

## About JIM

*"More than a Bean Counter"*

Most CPAs and other tax advisors operate in the after-the-fact world. Much like a score keeper in a baseball game, they can tell you what has happened, but have almost no input on making something happen.

Today more than ever individuals and small business owners need a true "Tax Bench Coach" to provide proper pro-active planning services. When one considers that taxes can claim up to 50% of any planned financial transaction, operating without knowing the tax ramifications, or without a viable tax minimization strategy, is just plain stupid.

James (Jim) Henderson, CPA is a graduate of the prestigious Boston Latin School, attended the University of Notre Dame, and graduated with high distinction from Babson College. He is a licensed CPA, Real Estate Broker and Notary Public. He has attended and presented numerous seminars on tax planning, real estate and home ownership, college planning, retirement planning, QuickBooks and other topics of interest to his clients and associates.

Jim, officially known as James A. Henderson, CPA, is the founder of Henderson, Grealis & Associates, PC CPA (aka *TaxSense*) with four offices in the Boston area. In addition to pro-active tax planning services, the firm, as Certified QuickBooks Pro Advisors, assists clients in making sense out of their numbers. "Information is power. Without *20/20* current and accurate financial statements, one cannot see where they've been, never mind see where they are going. As a result, proper tax planning becomes virtually impossible".

To learn more about Jim, please visit: TaxSense.com or contact him at (888) TAX-SENSE.

# CHAPTER 18

# Tips, Techniques and Little known Secrets of Real Property Ownership

*– Still the greatest "Tax Shelter" in the Internal Revenue Code*

By John E. Walters, MBA, EA

**M**onday morning, just after 9:00 am, the office phone rings, it's my longtime client Joe (we'll call him Joe because that is *not* his 'real name'). He was calling with great excitement in his voice and said, "I just pur chased my first investment rental property over the weekend and I need to see you right away to discuss the tax benefits of my investment."

"Okay Joe, let's meet tomorrow at 10:00 am in my office. I'll need you to bring a few things to our meeting. Please bring the big package that you received when you closed on the purchase of the new property and in particular the 'Settlement' statement that you received from your lender."

"Great!" Joe said, "tomorrow it is…see you then."

As I hung up the phone with him, I was mentally planning our meeting discussion set for the very next day and all the benefits the Tax Code offers to ownership of investment property

Acquiring The Property
**Analysis of the Settlement Statement**

*The Planting of the Early Tax Savings Seeds*

The next day, promptly at 10 am, Joe arrived at my office, eager and excited to discuss his new investment property.

"So let's take a look at that settlement statement that you brought with you," I said, as he pulled out the lengthy statements from a large folder that the mortgage company gave him and then he handed it to me. "Joe," I said, "this document tells us the story about what you just purchased and it also contains a wealth of Tax Savings related information that will get you on the right track to all the great benefits of your investment property ownership. Are you ready to review it together?"

Joe gave me a nod of agreement. "For the first step, we will look at the settlement costs or expenses from your **Form HUD-1** *settlement statement* that you were responsible to pay for as the buyer of the property and how they relate to your present and future tax benefits," I said. From the buyer's column of the HUD-1 we reviewed the numbered rows and columns, and I related to Joe how each was either a tax benefit to him now or would be in the future - when he sold or disposed of the property.

## Table 1

| Form HUD-1 | Settlement Costs and Expenses | Tax treatment for property Buyer |
|---|---|---|
| Row lines 100 - 600 | Real Estate Taxes City/Town/County | Deductible beginning on the date of Sale |
| Row lines 100 - 600 | Assessments, Condo and Assoc. Fess | Deductible beginning on the date of Sale |
| Row lines 700 – 704 | Real Estate or Broker Commissions | Amortize over Term of the Loan |
| Row lines 801 – 802 | Loan Origination fees or Loan discount (Points) | Amortize over Term of the Loan |
| Rows 803 – 811 | Items payable in the connection of the loan i.e. appraisal etc. | Amortize over Term of the Loan |
| Rows 901 | Interest | Deductible beginning on the date of Sale |
| Rows 902 – 905 | Items required to be paid in advance such insurance policies | Deductible beginning on the date of Sale |
| Rows 1000 – 1008 | Reserve deposits with lender | Not Deductible |
| Rows 1100 – 1113 | Items payable in connections with the title charges | Increase basis and are capitalized |
| Rows 1200 – 1205 | Government recording and transfer charges | Increase basis and are capitalized |
| Rows 1300 – 1305 | Additional settlement charges i.e. surveys, pest inspections, etc. | Increase basis and are capitalized |

"As you can see Joe, from Table 1, there are quite a few costs and expenses that you have paid in connection with your purchase, some we can use now on your present year tax return, and some will benefit you far into the future when you sell the property. I'm sure by this time you have realized just how important saving this document is, and that it needs to be safely maintained while you own this investment."

"Sadly," I said, "many clients have come to me in the past when they wanted to sell their investment property and they have not kept their settlement documents from when they purchased their property, and in-turn lose many of their *valuable* benefits and ultimately end up paying more in taxes than they needed too."

Upon ending our review of the Settlement statement I looked at Joe and said, *"We will not let this happen to you."*

"Now, are you ready to take the next step and put your new investment to work for you?" Again Joe eagerly nodded in agreement, and I relayed to him that I call this the first step:

## STEP 1
### SETTING UP THE PROPERTY FOR ACTIVE AND OPERATIONAL USE
### &
### GETTING IT "RIGHT THE FIRST TIME" FOR MAXIMUM BENEFIT

First, we are going to fill out a *Rental Property Setup Worksheet* using the information from your Settlement statement and in particular we'll use the following:

- Property Description, for example. 'Rental Condo'.
- Property Location, i.e. address of Investment/Rental property.
- Date Placed in Service, i.e. date that your property is available and ready to rent.

"This last item is very important since it will help us in establishing the date to start *depreciating* your new property."

Joe looked puzzled; he asked, "What is depreciation?"

"Joe, I'm glad you asked. *Depreciation* – in its most basic definition provides a means according to the Tax Code a way to deduct or (reduce) the cost of a capital asset (in your case the investment property you bought) over a specified recovery period expressed in years. To depreciate your new investment property correctly we will need to allocate the basis (total costs paid to acquire your investment property), i.e., cost of the building and the cost of the land, which, by the way, is not depreciable. Since we are on the subject of depreciation, you'll want to know that according to the present Tax Code the life of your property building is **27.5** years."

"That's quite a long time" said Joe, "I might not even own the property for that many years."

"Well," I replied. "In that case; we may want to *supercharge* your depreciation expenses to get the most benefit right now, by using a technique to separate the "real" property from the "personal" property of your investment, which is known as *cost segregation*. By using this technique, we are not only following the rules laid out in the Tax Code but we are reducing the "tax" lives of certain "personal" property of your investment to accelerate your deductions now, reduce your current tax liabilities, and increase your present cash-flow."

"Okay, that sounds good to me, when do we start?" said Joe.

"Well," I added, "since the subject of cost segregation can be very complex... we will have to save the complex details for a later discussion. But for now, let's look at some of the other expenses and fees you have pre-paid on your settlement statement that we can use in our worksheet; property taxes paid, pre-paid homeowners insurance policies, home owners association fees and amortization of your loan origination fees, and loan discount points."

"Are you ready to get to the next step?" I said to Joe.

"Sure" he replied.

I call this the second step:

## STEP 2
### Your first year in operation and beyond
### &
### Harvesting the 'annual' tax savings
### benefits during your ownership

"For this step, we will want to once again review your Settlement statement and Table 1 information for your recurring annual expenses such as; Mortgage payments, Property taxes, Property insurance, Condo & Management fees etc. Joe, do you recall at the beginning of our discussion today, I mentioned the importance of record keeping of all the documents relating to your investment?"

"Yes, I certainly do," said Joe.

"Well now," I said. "I am going to give you a booklet that you can use to record and save all the *income* and *recurring expenses* relating to your investment. So first, let's talk about the *income* you will be receiving as rent or lease payments from your tenants which you will report each year as *'passive'* income."

"Why is it called passive income?" asked Joe.

"Well, I'm glad you asked. It's called *"passive"* income since you did not have to *earn it as you would other types of income such as your* wages from employment. You will probably also receive a *"security" deposit* payment from your tenants when they first occupy your property, but this payment is not considered reportable and taxable income to you if it is a *"refundable" payment* to your tenants when they complete their lease or rental agreement with you. Now, let's talk about the *recurring* expenses that you might have while your property is "in service" and occupied by your tenants."

Since the categories of expenses can be rather extensive and specific to the type of property, here is a list of typical Investment or Rental property expenses:

| | | | | | |
|---|---|---|---|---|---|
| √ | Mortgage Payments | √ | Property Taxes | √ | Insurance |
| √ | Management Fees | √ | Utilities | √ | Landscaping |
| √ | Wages and Salaries | √ | Advertising | √ | Cleaning & Maintenance |
| √ | Commissions | √ | Improvements | √ | Legal & Accounting |
| √ | Repairs | √ | Supplies | √ | Depreciation |
| √ | Security | √ | Auto & Travel | √ | Pest Control |

"Of course, you may not have "all" of these *types* of expenses and you may very well have some others not covered in this list. But we will determine what to include in this list each year that you own the property. The important thing to remember is that you will need to be a good *record keeper* so that you do not <u>lose</u> any of these valuable deductions," I said.

> **TAX TIP:** Before we leave the subject of expenses, I do want to mention the "special" attention that the Tax Code gives to the expense types: *repair* vs. *improvement.* In general, the Tax Code states that repairs are expenses we can fully deduct in the year that they occur whereas an *improvement* may need to be *capitalized* and deducted (depreciated) over many years, just like your building. We will have to determine these differences each and every year when we meet to review your records.

"One final note before we move on to the third and final step in our discussion today. If after we have included all the income that you have derived from the property and deducted all the expenses for the year results in a *loss*, then this *loss* is subject to the *"passive activities" loss* rules," I added.

> **TAX TIP:** The present Tax Code allows for these losses to offset other *non-passive* income from other sources (i.e. wages & salaries) within certain limitations. This can be a very valuable and beneficial way to reduce income from other sources and any tax liabilities you may have from year to year. Of course, as with any tax law there are exceptions to the *passive activity* loss rules for certain classes of entities and individuals.

"Now, let's project ourselves for a minute or two into the future to the day that you want to complete the sale or exchange of your investment property. Are you ready to see what happens then?" I said to Joe.

"Okay" he said, shaking his head.

I call this the third and final step:

## STEP 3
### FINAL YEAR IN OPERATION
### AND PROPERTY DISPOSAL
### &
### REAPING THE TAX SAVING BENEFITS
### OF AN INVESTMENT SALE

"Joe, since you and I have worked together throughout the ownership period of this property, I know that you have kept good records of all the activities with this property so now it is time to reap your rewards and let's look at the tax aspects of the property sale. We can explore the possibility of a *Like-Kind* property exchange and defer any taxes on the sale far into the future, possibly forever but this subject is just as complex as the subject of *cost segregation*, so we will leave that as a topic for a later discussion. As you will recall Joe, we had to originally set up your rental property and establish a basis for *depreciation* purposes and allocate some of the costs of the purchase to the building and some to the land. Now, as the property seller, you have a final sales price for your property. This is usually located on your seller's *Settlement Statement* just as when you bought the property so many years ago."

"Next we want to subtract from your sales price the "expenses" that you incurred to sell your property. When we subtract these selling expenses, we now have the "amount realized" from the property sale. But before we conclude what *"taxable"* gain or loss you may have on the sale we must calculate the "adjusted" basis in the property, and for that we will need to take a look at your original purchase *Settlement Statement* for the following items:

1. Expenses for acquisition (i.e. costs we had to capitalize)

2. List of capital improvements throughout your ownership period.

Now Joe, it's time to account for all those years of *depreciation* we took and benefitted from as the owner of the property. This will be subtracted from the "adjusted" basis as above to arrive at the property's final adjusted basis and the *"taxable"* gain or loss on the sale. One final note, if you had any "suspended" losses in the prior years of your ownership due to the *Passive Activity* loss limitations we will use them to offset any taxable gain that you may have on the sale."

As you can see, it can become quite complex to arrive at that "final" tax figure on the sale. By employing the help and advice of a Tax Professional with expert knowledge in Real Estate transactions can ensure you maximize your ownership benefits, and help you reduce any taxes on the transaction to the lowest levels possible.

When our meeting that day concluded, Joe realized that there was quite a bit more to his property investment than he once thought. With property logbook in hand, he departed the office with a commitment to "stay in touch" often regarding his new investment.

Would you like to receive the same benefits as Joe? Then feel free to contact the author of this chapter at: John@lewaltconsulting.com with your questions.

## About John

John E. Walters, BS, MBA, EA has been a tax practitioner for 24 years and is the founder of LeWalt Consulting Groupe, LLC. His practice focuses on developing tax and financial strategies for his varied and diverse US and International clientele.

He formed this accounting and financial services firm with a single purpose in mind: To provide his clients with the highest level of ***personalized, professional*** client service possible.

John holds an MBA in Finance and Accounting from Southern Polytechnic State University and a BS in Engineering from San Diego State University. He holds the FINRA Series 7 & 66 securities licenses. He is the past President of the FSEA Sun Coast Chapter of Enrolled Agents and a Graduate Fellow of the National Tax Practice Institute.

If you would prefer to develop a relationship with a Professional Accounting and Financial services firm that **wants** to know your name, and **understand** your ***unique*** needs... then get to know... **LeWalt Consulting Groupe, LLC.**

You can contact John at: john@lewaltconsulting.com with your questions.

# CHAPTER 19

# The Tax Savvy Divorce

### By Gary D. Kane, CPA, MSA

You and your spouse have decided that you no longer want to be married to each other. What are the things that you are concerned about? ...division of assets, child custody issues, alimony or maybe how you can prevent your spouse from getting an even piece of the marital pie. If you're like most people, income taxes are one of the last things that you consider if you consider them at all. Journalist and author, Nora Ephron once quipped, "Marriage is temporary but divorce is forever." The tax mistakes you make today will follow you for years to come. There are tax traps for the unwary and opportunities for the informed. The following are the six tax-savvy items to remember if you join the 50% of Americans who end up in family court.

## 1. Alimony Is Deductible As Long As It's Alimony

The golden rule of divorce is that the spouse with 'the greatest amount of gold' gets to pay alimony. The computation of the amount and term of the alimony varies by state, but the tax rule is always the same: alimony is deductible by the payor and is includible in the income of the recipient. The definition of alimony is relatively straightforward: a cash payment paid pursuant to a decree of divorce or separate maintenance that will terminate on the death of the payee. The decree cannot state that the payment is not alimony and the parties cannot live together. As simple as the requirements are, it is not uncommon to find marital litigants and their representatives agreeing to terms that result in the law of unintended consequences. The common errors are:

a. The payment doesn't terminate on death. Bad drafting by the lawyer that doesn't specifically state that the payments end on the death of the payee will result in the disallowance of the deduction. More often, the payee wants to make sure that, in the event of his or her death, the kids get the balance of the alimony award and will require that payments continue after the death of the payee with negative consequences to the payor. Since payments do not have to be made to the former spouse, payments on his or her behalf can be surprise alimony. For example, it is common for the court to order the husband to pay the former wife's mortgage payments. If the decree doesn't specifically exclude the payment from the computation of alimony, it is deductible by the former husband and income to the former wife.

b. Child support is not alimony and is not deductible. Payments disguised as alimony but are actually child support will, in almost all cases, fail the alimony test and not be deductible. If your goal is a tax deduction for the alimony, do not have the payment reduced based on a contingency related to the children such as their reaching the age of majority, finishing school, etc

c. Unallocated support is generally alimony. Brad and Angie are getting divorced. The judge has ordered that Brad pay Angie $10,000 per month in temporary support, but Angie's lawyer doesn't request that the payment be allocated between deductible alimony and non-deductible child support. The result is that Brad gets a big deduction and Angie gets a new lawyer.

d. Don't forget alimony recapture. There is a provision in the code that eliminates the benefit of "front-loading" alimony, the purpose of which is to prevent the recasting of a property settlement as alimony. Formulas exist in the code to determine whether a greater portion of the alimony has been in the first three years after the divorce. If you fail the recapture test, the payor will be required to pay tax on the excess in the third year after the marriage. Likewise, the payee will get an offsetting deduction. For example, at the completion of the divorce, Brad pays Angie $150,000 and he decides to take an income tax deduction for the entire amount because his lawyer told him he could. His lawyer forgot to tell him that a little surprise awaited him when he filed his return three years later and had to pay it all back, and, if the tax rates go up in the interim, Brad is going to be really surprised.

## 2. Let Your 'EX' Pay The Tax On The 401(k)

Distributions from a retirement account such as a 401(k) or an IRA are subject to tax and can be subject to a 10% penalty for early withdrawal. There are provisions in the Code that will allow the division of a retirement account in a divorce tax-free to the owner. A Qualified Domestic Relations Order or QDRO is an order by the court to pay a portion of the retirement account into the account of the former spouse or a dependent of the former spouse. If the rules are followed, the recipient will pay the tax on the distribution when it is paid. There is one other significant benefit to the use of a QDRO: a distribution to a former spouse or dependent, referred to as an alternate payee, will avoid the 10% penalty for early withdrawal of the funds from the account. So, for example, cash can be distributed to the alternate payee who may be in a lower tax bracket than the account owner. The net result is that a greater portion of the cash is available since the income tax paid is less and the 10% penalty is completely avoided. Even though the insertion of a QDRO is simple, the case law is replete with stories of people who liquidate their retirement accounts rather than ask their attorney to draft a QDRO. Not all lawyers are capable of drafting QDRO's but there are independent companies who prepare them.

## 3. You Pay For Them, You Deduct Them

The Internal Revenue Code provides for a deduction for each qualifying child. The Code also provides that in the case of divorced parents, the custodial parent gets the dependency exemption. The parent that has the child the greater portion of the year is considered to be the custodial parent. The IRS allows the custodial parent to release the claim to the exemption – by providing the non-custodial parent form 8332 or on a form that conforms to the designated IRS form. Nothing will substitute for the form 8332 or for a conforming agreement – not state law, not an order by the court and not even the faithful and timely payment of child support. The simple solution to this problem is to have the agreement affirmatively state that the non-custodial parent is entitled to the exemption for the children in language that conforms to the statute. The statement must, among other things, be signed by the custodial parent, specify the year or years for which the release is effective, state that the custodial parent will not claim the children and will not be conditioned on the payment of support or any other contingency. It must also provide for the name of the child, the year or years for which the claim is released, the name and social security number of the parents and it must be signed. Former spouses are generally more likely to sign an agreement at the completion of the divorce when there is a judge ordering them to sign. Once the ink is dry on the marital settlement agreement, the cost of obtaining a signature goes up dramatically. Thus, the best solution is to require the signature on the form when the final agreement is signed.

## 4. Tax Arbitrage

Arbitrage is the practice of taking advantage of a price difference between two or more markets in order to capitalize on the imbalance between the prices. The income tax rates are structured progressively, that is, as a taxpayer's income increases, he moves into higher tax brackets. So, for example, your first dollar of taxable income is taxed at 10% whereas the last dollar of taxable income might be taxed at a rate as high as 35%. For divorcing parties, the goal is to use the difference in the marginal rates to help pave the way for a settlement that is mutually beneficial. Alimony is usually paid by the spouse with the greater income. An experienced divorce lawyer or an accountant can compute the tax savings that can be used to help both parties meet their needs. The equitable distribution of the family's assets in a divorce can also be accomplished using the imbalance in the tax rates. The tax code provides that for purposes of determining gain or loss, the recipient of an asset received in a divorce settlement will have the same cost basis as the transferor. For purposes of the marital settlement, the current value is used to determine an equitable settlement. So high value, low cost assets can be given to the spouse with the smaller income and vice versa for the spouse with the greater income. For example, Brad gives Angie the $50,000 IRA which for income tax purposes is considered to have a zero cost basis. If Brad is in the 35% bracket and Angie is in the 15% bracket, the tax savings is $10,000 (35% minus 15% times $50,000) which is not a bad day at the track.

## 5. Don't Trust The Jerk You Just Got Rid Of

The story that most divorce lawyers hear on a regular basis from their clients is that their spouse is a thieving jerk (the TJ) who has been under-reporting his or her income for years. Then, after every issue in the divorce is settled, the TJ wants his or her 'ex' to sign a joint income tax return. The TJ even offers to sign an agreement holding the 'ex' harmless for any additional taxes that might be owed for any open year. If you file a joint income tax return with your spouse, you are jointly and severally liable for any taxes that are owed. But what happens if the former spouse has been a tax scofflaw who has grossly underreported his earnings or negligently failed to pay his tax obligation? The answer is that the IRS will attempt to collect the amount owed and will grab the money from you. So what should you do if you are faced with divorcing a thieving jerk? The obvious answer is to not file a joint return. The IRS is not bound by a *hold harmless* clause in a marital settlement agreement so your only option is to sue in family court to get your money back. Good luck with that strategy. DO NOT FILE A JOINT RETURN. The Jerk may have forged your name to a return which could be considered a validly filed joint return unless you immediately file a separate return and advise the IRS that your signature was forged. The final alternative is to seek *innocent spouse relief.* The Internal Revenue Code allows for you to divide your tax liability if you did not know and had no reason to know that the taxes were understated and it would be unfair to hold you responsible for the underpayment. In order to be granted *innocent spouse relief,* you have to file form 8857 with the IRS. Innocent spouse relief requires you to prove your case, and should only be used in cases where you violated the general rule.

Half of all marriages in the United States end up in divorce court and probably the majority of those are relatively straightforward. If you have substantial assets such as real estate or securities, an interest in a business or retirement plan or if your income is substantial enough to result in alimony, you should at a minimum seek out the advice of not only a seasoned divorce attorney, but also a CPA with experience in family law matters. Divorcing couples are dealing with emotional issues and cooler heads need to be involved. Remember the words of Nora Ephron and don't make a mistake that will haunt you forever.

## About Gary

Gary D. Kane, CPA, MSA received his BSBA with honors with a major in accounting from the University of Florida and has a Master of Science in Accountancy from the University of Central Florida. He has over thirty-five years of public accounting experience – consisting of four years with the international accounting firm of Alexander Grant (Orlando, Florida) and over thirty-five years as a partner in Kane & Associates in Winter Park, Florida. He was also an accountant with Chevron Oil Company in charge of fixed asset accounting for all oil and gas properties in northern Louisiana, Mississippi, Florida and Alabama.

Gary is the managing partner of Kane & Associates. His primary responsibilities include the planning and utilization of personnel, budgeting, cash flow management, and overall firm marketing. He has been responsible for the supervision, planning, and review responsibilities for all tax preparation and planning functions within the firm. He performs the final, technical review of all audit and review engagements. Gary has lectured widely on various aspects of income tax planning, business valuation, forensic accounting and personal financial planning. He has appeared on numerous local television shows and has appeared on national cable television program broadcast on the Satellite Program Network. With his background in tax and financial planning, he has been instrumental in assisting clients in the formation, implementation and management of several real estate ventures, beginning with the planning stage through the completion and ultimate management or sale.

Mr. Kane is a member of the American and Florida Institutes of Certified Public Accountants, the National Association of Certified Valuation Analysts and is an Accredited Business Valuator, a Certified Valuation Analyst and is Certified in Financial Forensics. He is past president of the Central Florida Chapter of the International Association for Financial Planning and has served as Chairman of its Board of Directors. He has been an adjunct professor at the University of Central Florida teaching intermediate accounting and has assisted the Small Business Development Center at the University of Central Florida in lectures on business acquisitions and accounting systems for small businesses.

Gary Kane is licensed as a CPA in the State of Florida and is a member of the Collaborative Family Law Group of Central Florida. For more than twenty years, he has assisted attorneys in numerous areas, including tax planning, litigation, business valuation, expert testimony and divorce settlements. He has testified as an expert witness in Brevard, Orange, Osceola, Seminole, and Volusia Counties and in Federal Court in the Middle District of Florida.

www.ingramcontent.com/pod-product-compliance
Lightning Source LLC
Chambersburg PA
CBHW031500180326
41458CB00044B/6651/J